13.95

About the B

D1551789

I was privileged to have the opportunity
When Civilians Manned the Ships. *His b*
of some of the difficult to believe episodes w
in "Hooligans Navy" aboard LSM 279.

> Richard S. Schatz, Major USAFR (Ret.)
> President, USS LSM-LSMR Association

The language is graphic and at times salty—that adds authenticity—
after all this story isn't about choir boys.

> Weldon D. Mays
> Author's Shipmate

I like the narrative style. . . . The work is neither strident nor self-
conscious, and the author comes across as a very interesting person.

> Gerry McCauley, Literary Agent
> Gerard McCauley Agency, Inc.

. . .This LSM's trials, characters and human stories have been humorously
and accurately captured as the ship went often in harm's way. This volume,
dimmed not a bit by the passage of time, will add a spirited, human
dimension to the literature of the naval war in the Pacific.

> John W. Huston, Major General USAF (Ret.)
> Professor Emeritus, United States Naval Academy

. . .Fortunately for us, Lt. Kehl has the memory and energy to recount a
fascinating collection of the vignettes. Not only are they interesting and
amusing reading, but for all of us who were there it is easy to recognize
the stories are authentic. This book is enjoyable reading for any man
who served on one of these strange little ships, and must reading for
those who weren't there but would like to know what it was really like.

> Rolf F. Illsley
> Historian, USS LSM-LSMR Association

And Join in Preserving a Piece of History

The National LSM-LSMR Association's major project is to place an LSM (Landing Ship Medium) at a museum site, anticipated to be in the New Orleans area, for viewing by this and future generations.

As a ship, the LSM represents the ultimate in WW II amphibious technology. A few saw action in Korea and Viet Nam, but the Navy ultimately disposed of all ships of this class. Several were purchased by the government of Greece which has agreed to give one to the LSM-LSMR Association for its stated purpose.

The Association is in the process of raising funds to effect that ship's return, and the author has pledged to divert all income from the sale of this volume, once publication costs have been recovered, to this worthy cause, known officially as the LSM4US Project. You too may contribute: make tax deductible checks payable to NSLMA, and send to Larry Glaser, 237 Duquesne Boulevard, New Kensington, PA 15068.

When Civilians Manned the Ships:

Life in the Amphibious Fleet during WWII

LSM 911 group at a Sally Rand performance in Key West. From left to right around the table: Irwin J. Weiss, Oehrn W. Koon, L. Nigrello, J. Cardosa, Jim Kehl, Bill Lawrence, A.S. Feldman, Elmer Wojcik, J. Shawhan, and Isaac Aldridge.

When Civilians Manned the Ships:

Life in the Amphibious Fleet during WWII

James A. Kehl

BRANDYLANE PUBLISHERS
White Stone, Virginia

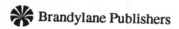 Brandylane Publishers

P.O. Box 261, White Stone, Virginia 22578
(804) 435-6900 or 1 800 553-6922; e-mail: brandy@crosslink.net

Copyright 1997, by James A. Kehl.
All rights reserved.
Printed in the United States of America.

Library of Congress Cataloging-in-Publication Data

Kehl, James A., 1922–
    When civilians manned the ships: life in the Amphibious Fleet during WWII/
James A. Kehl
    p.   cm.
    ISBN 1–883911–15–X
    1. Kehl, James A.   2. World War, 1939–1945—Amphibious operations.
3. World War, 1939–1945—Personal narratives, American. 4. Sailors–United
States–Biography. 5. United States. Navy—Biography.
I. Title
D769.45.K44 1997
940.54'5973—dc21

                                      97–7670
                                        CIP

TABLE OF CONTENTS

FOREWORD

Some fifty years after the events, it is refreshing to read a civilian's account of what life was like in the amphibious fleet during World War II. *When Civilians Manned the Ships* is just such a book—factual, believable, well-organized, and interestingly told from the viewpoint of one of the thousands of young men who abruptly changed his life style for the duration of a demanding and necessary war.

Told from experiences on board the Landing Ship Medium (LSM), it represents, to a marked degree, life aboard the Landing Ship Tank (LST) and the Landing Craft Infantry (LCI), all new ship concepts designed and built for the specific purpose of transporting and landing our armed forces and their equipment successfully on hostile shores.

The author artfully and at times humorously tells how this was accomplished in record time and how well the hastily indoctrinated civilians manned the ships. And the ships they manned were as new to the Navy as to their crews. There were no traditions to follow or records to break. For ships that were considered expendable, their record speaks for them.

How these snaproll, comfort-less, but capable ships got from here to there and back represents a tale that should be told and appreciated for having been told. After reading this one-of-a-kind book, I firmly believe that it deserves a wide readership among the public at large, especially among the descendants of the civilians who manned the ships. How better could a grandson or granddaughter learn what grandfather did in World War II than to read this most readable account? Three cheers for Lt. Kehl for taking the time and effort to set forth his memories!

Thomas A. Peacock, Cdr. USNR(R)
Commander, LSM Group 25

ACKNOWLEDGMENTS

Unable to locate all of my shipmates who are mentioned in this account and thereby seek permission to use their names, I have elected to use aliases for all of them. In recent years, several members of our crew have graciously supplied me with wartime records that have added to the work's authenticity. Ted Turner, Elmer Wojcik, Samuel News, and Oehrn Koon deserve my thanks for such support.

When members of other ships of our class (LSMs) learned that I was assembling my thoughts for this manuscript, they also supplied needed information. Eldon Smith, Joe Fields, James Silva, Rolf Illsley, and Kenneth Roberts all answered my questions and enlarged my knowledge of various topics.

During the war our group of LSMs was commanded by Thomas A. Peacock who answered to the code name of TOENAIL 25. Because he was our boss, he was frequently referred to as BIG TOENAIL by those of us with a love of parody. Now after more than a half century, at the age of 93, Commander Peacock has graciously undertaken to write the Foreword to this work, and I sincerely appreciate his input.

To more than any other, I am indebted to Weldon Mays, a trusted shipmate, who contributed numerous quotable quotes. In addition, he and Ken Roberts assumed the burdensome task of reading the entire manuscript while it was still in draft form, and both offered valuable suggestions for improvement. Errors that remain are mine alone—probably because I did not have the wisdom to interpret their comments.

I am also grateful to my wife, Barbara, who read my scribblings from the vantage point of an editor and to Pauline Kraly who assumed the laborious task of committing my words to the computer.

September 15, 1996   James A. Kehl

Introduction

Long before World War II, the United States Navy was hailed as the nation's first line of defense. Unfortunately with the outbreak of hostilities, even the fleet proved vulnerable and in need of protection. Any assumption of victory was premature without first conquering the sub-surface waters and the sky above. With an assist from reservists and volunteers, the Navy responded to that emergency by spectacularly upgrading its air and submarine branches to the point that the world has known no superiors.

The first phase of the fighting also isolated America and most of her allies on large land masses while the enemy defended similar areas separated by channels, straits, seas, and oceans. As another prelude to thoughts of victory, a means to engage the enemy had to be devised. The Navy responded to this challenge as well and quickly discovered that moving the Army and Marines, along with their weapons and supplies, onto hostile beaches required new technology. Translated into naval terms, this inspired the design and construction of amphibious-type vessels. Their ultimate emergence made the need for docks and harbors secondary in gaining a foothold in enemy-held territory and at the same time provided America with an awesome potential to invade anywhere in the world. (Quoted in *Alligator Alley*, hereinafter identified as *AA*, #17, p. 16.)

Although the gradual evolution of amphibious weapons and strategy moved forward, it lacked an essential ingredient: a nucleus of manpower similar to that which had spearheaded the development of the Navy's air and sub services. Thousands of landing ships and crafts rolled off assembly lines with no existing, formally trained personnel to man them. Although the regular Navy supplied the top administration, the ships and crafts were themselves staffed almost wholly by naval volunteers. Thus the newest branch, assigned the crucial task of placing the Army and Marines in position to engage the enemy, not only was dominated by volunteers but also possessed the least naval training.

Despite these handicaps, this group of men fought valiantly and can proudly claim for themselves the title, the Civilian Navy. These amphibious crews should not, however, be portrayed as groups of super-patriotic choir boys; remember, they were not assembled to sing lullabies to the Japanese invaders of the Pacific islands. Although commitment to the basic mission was always uppermost, individual traits often emerged to add color and excitement to our months together. In part, this individualized expression was so widespread because leadership had to be invented; the amphibious command could boast no background, no precedents, and no lore of its own. Thus the volunteers were in a unique position to carve out their own standards, often to the dismay of others both inside and outside the Navy.

Many of these civilians entered the service committed to carrying out their assignments as proficiently as possible, despite the fact that at times common sense had to be substituted for the vague and impractical orders received.

Others adopted a devil-may-care attitude, partly because of their adventurous natures and partly because of the widely circulated idea in the early days of the amphibious program that its men and ships were expendable. Occasionally these conflicting types clashed with each other or with regular Navy procedures. That inability to mesh, plus many personal idiosyncrasies and moral breakdowns brought on by the strains of war, spawned a behavior that at times could only be labeled as bizarre.

To some, the conduct of the Amphibious Force was indicative of an ambiguous farce, an impression ably illustrated by John C. Bird (LSM 156), who reported a completely civilian response in a ball-overboard incident. According to his account a group of twelve landing ships was traveling in a war zone where conditions were dangerous enough to warrant keeping half the crew at battle stations. During such group maneuvers, ships lost part of their ability to act independently; changes in speed, course, and how to engage the enemy in the event of attack were placed in the hands of the officer in tactical command (OTC).

Totally disregarding this subordination to the OTC, one of the ships suddenly pulled out of column and made a 180° turn. Alarmed at what seemed a dire emergency, the OTC requested an explanation and received a matter-of-fact message in response: "Our basketball has fallen overboard." That was supposed to be an adequate accounting to justify any erratic action. The ship went to retrieve the ball without any recognition that protocol had been breached. Reclaiming the basketball represented logic to the civilian mind and was undoubtedly crucial to the ship's extremely limited recreational program, but in the face of wartime conditions, the action potentially placed the whole convoy at risk. (*LSM-LSM(R) WW*

II Amphibious Forces, hereinafter cited as *LSM Amphibious Forces*, p. 70)

Amphibious life constituted a world of its own. Just as these ships were unique in function, the crews that manned them were equally distinctive—a spectrum of civilian types trying to homogenize their youthful non-experience, Navy regulations, and base training into a kind of fighting unit that had never before been assembled. As daring and committed as any who served during the war, amphibious personnel were more informal, unpredictable, and undisciplined than any other branch of the Navy.

Oftentimes, the greater the challenge, the greater the accomplishment. That describes the achievement of many who served in the Amphibious Force during the war. Inexperienced in the ways of the Navy, they confidently boarded newly-designed, untested ships to undertake, with distinction, the vital task of beach landings, which had never before been tried.

This work is not an attempt to analyze strategy or to assess the impact of the amphibians on the outcome of the battles in the Pacific. It is primarily a light and lively assessment of individuals: their quirks when confined, their ability to adapt to strange assignments and places, their conduct under pressure, and their responses to life-threatening situations.

Neither is this account a history of the Amphibious Force or any portion thereof. Based primarily on the author's recall after fifty years, plus his brief notes and a few assists from shipmates, this work still lacks the analytical and comprehensive quality of an authentic amphibious history. Although war details, specific dates, and ship information are accurate, they do not represent the focus; they only provide the setting for glimpses into personality—human actions and reactions under wartime conditions, as well as humorous incidents resulting from civilians being suddenly thrust into Navy lifestyles.

It is impossible to set forth a history based largely on recall unless the writer occupied a crucial leadership role that provided access to strategy and planned interactions. My colleagues and I enjoyed no such Mt. Olympus from which to view the Pacific war and experienced only an "in the trenches" perspective. We were making history, not writing it. Years later, one shipmate sagely explained: "Being only eighteen years old at the time, I did not consider that what we were doing was a real part of history. To be honest, until I was in my third year of college, it did not occur to me that being a part of those invasions was history."

Occasionally an author describes his work as "warts and all" in order to portray its comprehensiveness. This document is an attempt to invert the process, emphasizing the warts while relying on the history and narrative only to move from one wart to another. Each chapter is a different profile of amphibious life; thus the total adds up to a series of slices of dramatic, humorous, and irregular incidents, especially those bordering on the absurd. With equal clarity, these chapters may be read independent of each other and in any order.

To readers who demand complete accuracy, this volume presents two flaws: one author-induced and the other the aforementioned human frailty of recall. The former is the result of respect for the privacy of crew members and their families. On the one hand, nationally known persons who are only incidental to the narrative are properly identified; in all other instances the names have been changed to disguise identification; in several incidents, actions of two or three individuals have been attributed to one character in order to minimize the number

xiii

of cameo appearances. Even the number of the ship that provides the setting has been altered in the interest of privacy.

Because much of this volume relies on recollections, accuracy is always in doubt because recall is an unscientific approach, often more vivid than accurate. Certain individuals and statements, even those fifty years or more in our past, make indelible impressions and cannot be forgotten. At the same time in order to keep such situations fresh in our minds, we often depend on *selected* specifics and assign them more emphasis than warranted; as a result we tend to distort the original happening. After years of telling, retelling, enhancing, and forgetting, reality becomes garbled, often leaving members of the same crew with widely different versions. Furthermore, because any two reports of the same incident will produce conflicting descriptions, recall, both in fact and interpretation, becomes less and less exact as the years pass.

Although accuracy was always in the forefront of my thinking, I recognize that recall has these definite limitations. To my shipmates and other "Old Navy Salts," these pages should stimulate your own recall, perhaps at odds with mine in detail, but nonetheless similar in graphic impressions. All others are invited to share the bizarre experiences of a cadre of erstwhile civilians riding out the war on a ship that, when the sea was rough, resembled a bobbing cork in a bathtub.

CHAPTER I

We Too Have Tales to Tell

When *The Longest Day*, depicting the invasion at Normandy, was making its way around local movie houses, a teenager purportedly asked her father, a veteran of the landing, to accompany her to a viewing. He replied: "No, thanks. I was there for the stage version. That was enough."

My shipmates and I aboard the LSM 911 (the number has been changed to protect the guilty) could give the same response to a similar comment concerning *Mr. Roberts*. We lived out the theme of that stage and film classic years before it was written. Plagued by a petty, insecure prototype of Mr. Roberts' commanding officer (CO), we decided to produce a manuscript of our own. Randomly we jotted down outrageous incidents, quotations, and reactions in a journal that the executive officer squirreled away among his navigational charts.

None of the four officers fully appreciated the potential in the material we were collecting. One of us was trained as an engineer, one as an agriculturist, another as a business major, and I had graduated with credentials to teach history. All four had enlisted in the Navy directly from college, had no experience in our chosen professions, and were completely inept in the literary field. The only motivation for recording our experiences was that the rapport between us and the captain and between the crew and the captain was deteriorating rapidly, and we felt impelled to preserve our feelings for some undefined purpose, perhaps as a written record that we too had served. At the time it never crossed our minds (as it did the mind of the author of *Mr. Roberts*) that others in the Navy were troubled by similar misfortunes; as a result we feared that no one would identify with our plight.

On that assumption, one day after an incredulous incident with the captain (there were so many that I can't remember which one), the exec picked up our "tell-all" report and in frustration explained: "Look, guys, with this captain, we're never going to get back, and if by chance we do, no one will believe our story." Receiving no argument, he threw the journal over the side to end our writing careers before we had an opportunity to split an infinitive or dangle a participle. Never has a group of four bungled the assessment of a situation more completely than we did.

Nine years later under similar circumstances, Herman Wouk penned a similar lament in *The Caine Mutiny*. In anticipation of the courtmartial of the Caine's Captain Queeg, he prompted actor Fred MacMurray, alias the ship's communications officer, to conclude: "They'll never believe our story. . . . We won't be able to make it stick." With these words, he re-stated our fear, but there was a difference: MacMurray's timidity only delayed Queeg's loss of command, whereas our exec's action permanently shelved our effort to compile a documentary on our captain's misadventures.

2

Mr. Roberts and *The Caine Mutiny* captured the tempo and apprehension not only in our lives, but also in the lives of thousands of others and presented them in humorous and compelling classics that have thrilled millions. At this stage all that survives from our aborted project are a few personal memories that I now endeavor to record for posterity.

Today *Mr. Roberts*, with equal kudos to *The Caine Mutiny*, tops a distinguished list of vignettes of the World War II Navy published over the last fifty years. In compiling this literary calendar, authors and playwrights, along with TV and movie script writers, have accurately presented the wartime heroics, antics, and anxieties of shipboard life through storylines and settings featuring aircraft carriers, destroyers, submarines, supply ships, minesweepers, and even PT 109, while completely overlooking the amphibious force.

As a branch created in the war years to meet unique conditions, the amphibious Navy was more thoroughly dominated by reserves, otherwise known as civilian enlistees, than any other branch. In addition to their extraordinary functions, amphibious vessels encompassed all the romance and foibles found elsewhere in the naval service, an observation set forth here to highlight an untapped resource for the next wave of World War II writers.

Although the Caine's Queeg and Mr. Roberts' CO stand out as role models not to be emulated, the amphibs unfortunately can offer reasonable facsimiles; we served with one of them. No viewer will ever forget how the USS *Reluctant's* captain meticulously nurtured several potted palms outside his cabin, and how in utter frustration at the end of the novel, Mr. Roberts' friend, Ensign Frank Pulver, pitched those damned scrubby plants overboard, boasting defiantly of the deed to his captain. To me and my fellow crew members aboard the 911, that captain and Queeg will always remain as real and as much a part of the Navy as Admirals Nimitz and Halsey.

Our CO, Lester Smarba, did not replicate the *Reluctant's* horticultural tendencies on the LSM 911, but did acquire his own fetish that we labeled *the deck chair syndrome*. It emerged instantly on a blistering hot afternoon in the South Pacific as we passed an LCI (Landing Craft Infantry) on which life seemed ridiculously out of character for wartime. Admittedly the sight was a spectacle to behold: sailors with cold drinks in hand, sporting shorts, sunglasses, and broad-brimmed straw hats and lounging about on brightly striped canvas deck chairs, the modestly priced kind available in season in any Sears or J.C. Penney store.

Smarba was immediately smitten by the deck chair image and committed himself to the proposition that it must be duplicated on the 911. At the time I didn't know if the acquisition of chairs was expected to divert our minds from the seriousness of the war or to promote the impression that we were on an extended Love Boat vacation at the expense of the federal government, or if the chairs were desired solely for the captain's own gratification. Whatever the reason, procurement was assigned the highest priority; it took precedence over the defeat of Japan and temporarily even surpassed in importance the captain's quest for dill pickles.

The 911 storage compartment contained an adequate allotment of both sweet and sour pickles to complement any culinary delight our cooks could create, but the captain had a specialized craving for dill pickles that could be satiated by no other pickle. If he had been a woman, we would have become suspicious; two invasions later, we acquired a case, and he celebrated their arrival by devouring three large dill strips with his creamed chicken dinner; the combination was as unappetizing as anchovies served with hot pear juice or beer poured over cornflakes. But for the moment, deck chairs pushed the dictates of his palate into second place.

As the commissary and stores officer, I was at the forefront of both the pickle chase and the chair search. I thought that the odds on the chair acquisition were greater than the chances of the Navy ever locating Amelia Earhart. Repeatedly when I prepared to pick up supplies, the captain treated me like an errand boy, summoning me to his presence and posing the same ridiculous question: "Are you sure you have a signed requisition for deck chairs?" Occasionally, but not too often over this period, he also asked about my being prepared to requisition dill pickles. To my affirmative reply, he always answered "good!" with an air of anticipation, taking for granted that I was fully equipped with the proper documentation to procure such "non-essentials" to our mission as food, maintenance supplies, and paint.

The chair search seemed hopeless, primarily because none of the long string of atolls where we anchored had a Sears or Penney's franchise, but the captain never gave up hope. After all, that LCI had to have acquired its chairs somewhere, and the captain wasn't accepting my argument that perhaps an enterprising individual had purchased them with his own money in the states before being ordered overseas.

It became increasingly embarrassing to inquire about deck chairs; supply officers looked at me in disbelief, as though I were in a time warp with no knowledge that a war was underway. After numerous humiliating discussions with supply people that spanned several months, the exhausting search

5

seemed about to reach a happy ending. As we readied to go alongside a supply barge off Tulagi, the captain's binoculars spied a number of deck chairs glistening in the sun on the deck of the barge. When Columbus's sailors sighted land, they couldn't have been more jubilant than Smarba was at that moment. At first he thought it was a mirage and asked me to confirm his long-sought after pot of gold, chair-shaped and canvas-covered. His identification was unmistakable; the chairs shone brightly against the background of a white bulkhead. He almost rammed the barge in his haste to get me to the supply officer before the representative from the ship that was simultaneously mooring on the other side; he knew instinctively that the other vessel was intent upon snatching *his* deck chairs before I got there.

Boarding the barge, I won the race to the supply desk, only to hear the disheartening report: "There are no deck chairs available." We had successfully located the source of the LCI's Rest and Relaxation (R&R) equipment, but the supply had been exhausted months before. Unwittingly, the few chairs on deck had toyed with the captain's emotions; he was revved up to the point that he could already feel himself sinking into one, but that wasn't to be. The chairs were not a false advertisement of wares for distribution but were reserved for the leisure hours of the barge's own personnel. With that explanation I concluded my other business and returned to the 911, leaving several sailors to transfer the supplies I had requisitioned.

On entering the wardroom (officers quarters), I was prepared to impart the sad news, but before I could speak, the captain rushed over to me and shook my hand—the only time that ever happened, except when he had welcomed me aboard as a member of his staff five months before. I was dumbfounded at this show of affection, particularly in the face of failure, and hastened to explain that I had struck out again. Smarba thought that I was jesting; I can't imagine why because I never joked with him, but he insisted: "You can't fool me; I saw two come aboard." Because he was deadly serious when he spoke, I knew that he had misinterpreted what he saw.

I sought out the sailors assigned the detail of moving our supplies from the barge to the 911. One confided that "accidentally on purpose" two chairs from the deck of the barge were commingled with our supplies and carried across with them. Hiding around the corner and inside a companion way, the captain observed what he thought was a legitimate transfer. When I reported back that, in effect, our ship was the recipient of stolen goods, the captain's chin dropped.

Gloom had replaced joy. He was almost uncontrollably disappointed—not that the men had heisted the chairs, but that the crew had them and he didn't. He summoned his brain cells into executive session and soon expounded a little philosophical nonsense. Smarba reasoned that the theft reflected on the ship, particularly on him as captain. If an inquiry were ever held, he would be called on to answer for the conduct of his crew. He was willing to assume that responsibility for a price: namely, one of the chairs. If the crew agreed to gratify him in this one detail, he was prepared to bear the onus and would not prosecute anyone for stealing. After working his way through this twisted logic for the officers, he concluded: "Fair is fair; I only want one chair. I'm not trying to be a complete shit about this," but unfortunately he aspired to be at least a half.

Once we left the confines of Tulagi, the sailors responsible for finding the chairs before the barge had lost them intended to put them on deck for the enjoyment of all hands.

7

That explanation was presented to the captain and promptly rejected. He had permitted the chair syndrome to take command of his mind to the extent that he couldn't live with anything less than a chair with the word "captain" printed across the back. In response, the crew surrendered all interest in both chairs. They were placed on the starboard superdeck, outside the captain's sea cabin, and one was labeled as the captain had dictated.

To register our total disgust, no member of the crew and no officer, aside from the captain, ever sat in either chair. I have no idea what their ultimate disposition was, but I assume that they met the same fate that Ensign Pulver visited on his captain's potted palms.

CHAPTER 2

The Day of the Landing Ship

At the outset of World War II, the Japanese had captured the archipelago from their homeland to the Solomon Islands. Part of the MacArthur plan to reclaim that territory and power the United States to victory was a strategy known as island hopping—invading some while bypassing others. To achieve this goal, the Americans were required to undertake dozens of landings on hostile shores, some of which were more spectacular conquests than others.

Unfortunately, in the early months of the conflict, the Navy did not possess landing ships and crafts designed specifically to deliver Army and Marine units to enemy-held beaches. This vacuum dramatized the need for an amphibious fleet, a need that the Navy undertook to design and build at a rapidly accelerating pace.

Because such vessels were smaller and less complex than those in the battle fleet, contracts were quickly extended to shipbuilding companies in ocean, gulf, and river ports. Landing Ship Tanks (LSTs) and Landing Ship Mediums (LSMs) were

9

launched by the hundreds, whereas the smaller landing craft were fabricated in even more staggering numbers. Between April 1944 and February 1946, an unbelievable 494 LSMs were commissioned; in addition, sixty were modified to fire rockets (LSMRs). Every week over that period, the fleet was enlarged by a combination of five LSMs and LSMRs. Contracts were let to six companies, all of which established phenomenal records for efficiency, with the most LSMs being launched by the Brown Shipbuilding Company of Houston. Many others, including our 911, were constructed in the Charleston Navy Yard.

From the laying of the keel to launch required one month of construction time, and a similar period was needed to carry an LSM to commissioning. Although the first one built (the 201) took considerably longer to complete, assembly line techniques gradually swung into place to achieve this rapid construction. The life span for most of these two-month marvels in the U.S. fleet proved to be approximately two years, not because they were obsolete or worn out, but because the war ended. Many were later refitted and functioned in the service of foreign governments or in private ventures, and a few still operate today. (*LSM Amphibious Forces*, pp. 17-18.)

This expansion created new demands both for thousands of men and for a separate Navy subdivision, a need that brought to prominence Admiral Richmond Kelly Turner, who headed the Administrative Command, Amphibious Forces of the Pacific Fleet (AdComPhibsPac). Manpower, in both the officer and enlisted ranks, for this new command was supplied almost exclusively by volunteers with no Navy background. As a result of this expansion, an estimated 35,000 men, mostly civilians, served aboard LSMs during the last sixteen months of the Pacific war.

In commenting on these crews, Admiral Daniel E. Barbey, then commander of the Seventh Amphibious Force, observed that: "New ships mean new crews, but I was hardly prepared to find that the total sea experience aboard most of the beaching ships was just about zero. I do not mean combat experience; I mean enough experience to go aboard a ship and take her from here to there." (Quoted in *AA*, #19, p. 16.) Gradually the Navy leadership in general joined Admiral Barbey in expecting the unexpected from the civilians who manned these ships.

I was among the volunteers assigned to one of these Navy miniatures, an LSM about two-thirds the length of a football field (203.5 ft.). Much smaller than an LST (by 125 ft.), it was much faster, with a top speed of twelve knots unless assisted by a strong tail wind. Despite this modest rate of progress over the waves, it possessed the most powerful engines in the amphibious fleet. Designed with the same Fairbanks Morse or General Motors diesels as the destroyer escort, the LSM could never achieve the same speed because of its flat bottom, a condition necessary to facilitate beach landings. Drawing only three feet at the bow and six and a half feet aft when empty, an LSM was a veritable cork unleashed to ply the oceans of the world.

This shallow draft, although designed to facilitate landings, also served as part of an LSM's defense at sea. The enemy's surface vessels presented no serious threat by the end of 1944, but attack from aircraft and submarines was still real. Most LSMs were armed with a 40 mm at the bow and four 20 mm guns around the superdeck to repel strafing runs, but they continued to be vulnerable to torpedo assault from both the air and the sea. Fortunately, it was impossible to set a torpedo shallow enough to hit an LSM, but that did not stop the

Japanese from trying; several ships reported such attacks, with the torpedo passing underneath and harmlessly out to sea.

Potentially, a submarine offered a more serious threat if it surfaced. Its greater firepower permitted it to stand out of range of our guns, with the possibility of ultimately destroying us if it dared to remain exposed on the surface long enough to do so. Instructed in how to respond if surprised by a surfaced sub, we were advised to head toward it, ram it if possible (an enemy sub for an LSM was regarded as a good exchange), and at all costs sweep the sub's personnel off its deck with gunfire before they swung into action.

By the close of World War II, the LSM represented the ultimate in amphibious ship technology. Monumental casualties on the coral reefs of Tarawa (Gilbert Islands) in late 1943 had been the determining factor in the Navy push for a new type of amphibious assault ship, one that in appearance suggested a deformed hybrid of all previous designs. Something faster and more maneuverable than the LST, as well as something with a greater range than the LCI, was urgently needed. Combining features from both and adding innovations gleaned from experience, the LSM came off the drawing board and onto the sea.

With a range of 8,000 miles without refueling, with an ability to sustain both the crew and forty-five to fifty assault troops for at least three weeks, and with a turning circle that permitted a 360° turn in its own length, this "ugly duckling" took its place in the fleet. Not emerging as a tested reality until after D-Day in Europe, the LSM became a uniquely Pacific phenomenon. It made its combat debut on the beaches of Leyte on October 20, 1944, and assisted General MacArthur in fulfilling his "I shall return" pledge. From that date forward, it was an integral part of the strategy that landed ships on every

12

major beachhead (Luzon, Iwo Jima, and Okinawa) and that anticipated the invasion of the Japanese homeland.

Another distinguishing feature of the LSM was its main deck; comprising eighteen feet of the ship's 34.5-foot beam and extending the full length of the vessel, it was designed to carry such motorized equipment as tanks and trucks. During the assault on Lingayen Gulf, the 911, for example, carried five medium tanks, one bulldozer, two jeeps, and two Piper cubs with their wings detached and the separate parts mounted on the jeeps, plus the personnel to man this combination of vehicles. For the Okinawa invasion, we transported a medical unit: jeeps, ambulances, and supplies. During the initial phases of an invasion and between invasions, LSMs were assigned to ferrying men and supplies from island to island and from transports anchored two or more miles off shore to the beach. On such short runs from ships in the harbor to the beach, these vessels could carry more than 500 tons per trip. (A.D. Baker, III, ed., *Combat Fleets of the World*, (Annapolis: U.S. Naval Institute) p. 62)

LSMs were constructed with their navigational stations (radio, radar, chart room, helm, and bridge) on the starboard side amidships. As the LSM's most distinctive feature, this cylindrical superstructure was novel enough to render the ship an object of ridicule, at times by its own personnel. One sailor described his ship as a shoe box with a tin can mounted on it, and those on another were more picturesque in their imagery, depicting theirs as a Floating Shit House. Carrying that designation a step further, they designed a logo that was tastefully painted on the conning tower; it pictured a raft adorned by an outhouse and a miniature cannon. (George C. Floersch, *AA*, #6, p. 5)

To me, the symbolism was still different: a bathtub with a periscope, but on the horizon, this structure presented the silhouette of a 1940s vintage aircraft carrier; when an LSM closed within a mile, that deception was unmasked; it resembled an oversized, old-fashioned bathtub submerged slightly above the feet. In rough seas, no one dwelt on this bathtub appearance because the ship's cork-like movement became all-consuming. In the end, after being rolled, tossed, and pitched for more than 50,000 miles in less than two years aboard one of these "untamed broncos of the sea," most of us agreed that it was unsinkable, but we would have preferred to bypass the demonstration.

Those who came to know an LSM intimately can readily identify with the floating bathtub image. The stern was squared off like the end of a tub that contains the fixtures; the bow, comparable to the curved back of its bathtub predecessor, was constructed with two hydraulic doors that swung open to expose a sturdy, steel ramp that could be lowered to land men and vehicles from the main or tank deck onto the beach. This awkwardly shaped, though highly functional, ship was the antithesis of what most of us expected when we joined the Navy; it defied the aesthetic, trim-lined image of Navy vessels pictured in our grade school history books.

At anchor, a landing ship stood in sharp contrast to capital ships, partly because the latter were secured in place by bow anchors. On LSMs, bow anchors were only auxiliary in nature, limited almost exclusively to emergency use. Primary reliance was assigned to anchors dropped from the stern; as a result, LSMs at anchor looked as though the ocean had seized them by their tails and they were straining to work themselves free.

Dangled at the end of a cable (not a chain), a stern anchor was an integral part of the ship's design. When assuming this new mission of delivering men and supplies to the beach, the landing ship required some means, more readily available than

14

the next flood tide, to retract itself from the mud, sand, or coral that had halted its progress at or near the water's edge during the beaching maneuver. To provide such a means of withdrawing from the beach, a landing ship dropped its stern anchor 450-600 feet off shore (before it expected to run out of ocean). In order to retract the ship from its grounded position, a stern anchor engine reeled in the cable, which had the effect of pulling the ship back toward the anchor until it was once again afloat.

Almost everyone assigned to LSMs suffered an inferiority complex to some degree. The smallness of the ship and the fact that few of us had been to sea before were major factors in shaping this attitude. With fifty-four men and five officers, the 911 could count only four who had experienced sea duty; that was hardly a confidence builder to the rest of us as we prepared to face the enemy, but it was a higher ratio than many LSMs enjoyed.

The most popular and talkative of the four was the gunner's mate, who had served aboard a battleship at Pearl Harbor on the day of infamy. We must have sucked out of him every drop of information about sea life that he had accumulated. As I reflect on the circumstances, his insights were not particularly relevant because he knew nothing more about amphibious duty than we did; but in the kingdom of the blind, the one-eyed is king. Even though his area of special knowledge was the surprise attack and its devastation, we tried to glean what we could, but it wasn't much on which to base an optimistic view of the future.

When most of us had enlisted, we knew little about the Navy's overall operation. Our understanding was limited to books and movies that had exaggerated the role of the battle fleet—where a high percentage of us had expected to serve. Once assigned to the amphibious force, we lived in the shadow of the big ship navy that we thought we had joined. Throughout the war, I never caught a glimpse of a battle fleet deployed for action.

The closest I came was a memorable moment when a single battleship, the *New Jersey*, under a full head of steam, passed the 911 off the coast of Samar. The sight was majestic and awesome—like a portable fortress gracefully plying a path before our eyes toward an unknown rendezvous. Afterward I could only reflect on our less glamorous duty. Unlike larger ships, those of the amphibious fleet didn't even have names—only numbers. If the term *identity crisis* had been in vogue at the time, a therapist would undoubtedly have diagnosed me with having a terminal case. We lacked the aura of dignity associated with duty aboard a *New Jersey*, *South Dakota*, or *Enterprise*; we could only write home to report that we were aboard a number. (Even fictional ships such as Mr. Roberts' *Reluctant* and Captain Queeg's *Caine* were more than numbers.) No one was eager to report that he was aboard "a Pacific Puddle Jumper" or, as I have shown, something even more demeaning. We all knew the popular terminology.

Although personnel on landing ships enjoyed many advantages not shared by those pulling duty on larger ones, our morale was acutely affected by the lack of certain amenities. We did not possess a single Coke machine, were issued no movie projector, were not equipped with an ice cream maker, and could boast of no full-scale Small Stores (where clothing, candy, tobacco products, shaving gear, and other toiletries could be purchased).

For the most part, we were at the mercy of Navy bases and larger ships for such conveniences. When we moored alongside vessels with a Small Stores facility, it was opened to our men if convenient. When invited aboard, men from amphibious ships such as ours tended to raid the candy shelves until they resembled Old Mother Hubbard's cupboard unless limiting stipulations were applied. To preserve a reasonable supply of goodies for their own crews, large ships were reluctant at times to entertain predators like us aboard. When they shut the door to us and a significant percentage of our sailors were in need, the denial was a ready-made basis for complaint. Rumblings of second-class citizenship temporarily echoed through the ship until our attention was drawn to something more substantive.

Large ships were as cooperative as their own situations would permit. On one occasion a destroyer, realizing our limitations, offered a three-gallon container of vanilla ice cream with the single stipulation that the container be returned. That generosity provided each of us with less than half a pint of the manna we had craved over the five months since our last such treat, but we could all write home: Today we had ice cream for dessert.

Shortly thereafter, we realized that a lack of ice cream wasn't the greatest food calamity to be endured. When a PT boat pulled alongside and the two crews exchanged greetings and information, our men learned that PTs didn't even have galleys and that their personnel were at the mercy of other ships for all hot meals, a condition that LSM sailors took for granted and enjoyed at least once, if not two or three times a day. Although we couldn't return the favor to the destroyer, we could follow its example of thoughtfulness by inviting the PT crew to a hot meal. Once extended, our invitation was also good for our morale; when we complained about being deprived of a Small Stores outlet, we could recall that PT boats lacked our dining facilities, an advantage we treasured daily.

A deficiency that was particularly vexing to me was the absence of a motorized small boat to reach the shore from the distant anchorage where we were invariably assigned in almost every port. The oar-powered wherry included as part of the standard equipment was almost useless; the distances that we had to travel in most harbors were generally far beyond the range of a rowboat. No one considered deploying the wherry even for the most routine tasks.

Picking up mail or supplies or sending the crew on liberty always placed us at the mercy of the seemingly random schedules followed by the boats servicing the harbor. At times we desperately needed the exclusive use of a boat because the volume of supplies or the number of men expecting liberty was such that we could not share; but gaining even temporary use of a boat required reaching shore to make the necessary arrangements. Nothing seemed to be a greater waste of time than waiting for the harbor boats, but the Navy brass probably thought we had nothing more constructive to do at that time, and they were right.

Thus, with their uncomely appearance, logistical warts and all, LSMs came to dot Pacific harbors and beaches and, along with other amphib units, helped to push the war ever closer to the Japanese homeland, but it was one rough ride all the way.

The Shining Sea Myth

While the LSM 911 was still thousands of miles from the Pacific war zone, the crew was already under attack from its most relentless enemy, the sea. At the outset, we lacked confidence in our ocean-going cork's ability to stay afloat as normal corks always do; we doubted that it could withstand the punishment that the sea was capable of meting out. With every tempest, the battle was joined anew, and on every such occasion throughout its twenty-one months of naval service, the 911 rose to the challenge by refusing to surrender to the worst storms the ocean could brew.

18

During our first voyage (from Charleston to Norfolk), the LSM proved that it was a worthy combatant for the boisterous waves that crashed across its bow. A more crucial question was: Could the crew survive the duel between ship and sea. That first trip served notice that we had not embarked on a tranquil cruise, because repeatedly the two went toe-to-toe, and members of the crew absorbed body blow after blow in the struggle to retain control of both the ship and our physical well-being. Gradually we bowed to the evidence that the ride was destined to be rough, but our worst projections did not hint that we would be compelled to fight the weather for a large portion of our 50,000-mile pilgrimage at sea.

Engineering calculations revealed that an LSM was constructed to roll left and right through a larger arc than any other ship of the fleet and not capsize. At times our hope of survival rested squarely on faith in that statistic. Confronted with no tangible proof that the next wave would not cast us into Davy Jones's locker, we were little more than hostages when the Goliath of the sea and our technological cork squared off in their periodic duels. In typhoons, ship-handling was almost an exercise in futility because the sea dictated course and speed. Although no one was measuring, the LSM rolled through a thirty-degree arc, but those experiencing the ride swore that range was closer to sixty-eighty degrees. To make the ride even more jarring, the LSM was engineered with a snap roll—meaning that in high seas the ship moved from an extreme right to an extreme left position and back every eight to ten seconds. That jerked the crew to and fro with sickening regularity for as much as five continuous days—an effective, but not prescribed, means of promoting weight loss for the unwilling participants. When I arrived in the Chesapeake from Charleston, I thought that I had already lived three days longer than my stomach.

The Day of the Landing Ship

On the return trip south from Norfolk, we learned for a second time why Cape Hatteras bears the ominous title, "the graveyard of ships." Off that North Carolina coast, we encountered a more punishing storm than we had experienced when headed north. From the continuous pounding that the ship absorbed from the waves, it sprung a leak between a fuel tank and the fresh water supply, and we couldn't pump water for drinking or for galley use without the taint of oil.

When a sailor went to the scuttlebutt to quench his thirst, an odoriferous mixture greeted his senses of taste and smell as it swished by his tonsils. Cooks drawing water for cooking also had to contend with the unsavory combination. At noon the next day the green beans glistened with droplets of oil on every particle. To counteract this contamination of our water supply, we substituted juices for water whenever possible, but coffee brewed with pineapple juice just didn't deliver the wake-up call that sailors expected. Likewise dry cereal, activated by a concoction of powdered milk and grape juice, was not appetizing even to the least discriminating palate.

On the positive side, the pharmacist's mate reported a complete absence of patients coming to sickbay complaining of constipation, but he armed himself with an abundance of a Kaopectate equivalent in anticipation of the steady stream of anxious new patients who crossed his threshold. To minimize the expected physical discomfort and to repair the leak with dispatch, we altered our course from a Canal Zone heading in favor of an emergency stop at Key West.

In Norfolk, the 911's new executive officer had come on board, and this was his first adventure in the open sea aboard our cork. Months later, he confided to me that he never expected to reach port alive. Although he had been to sea on a small aircraft carrier, he had never experienced the snap roll before. Like most of us over the months that followed, he gradually became a believer, accepting the premise that an LSM would stay afloat under the most hazardous conditions even though it mercilessly punished its crew in the process.

Believers that we were, our faith wasn't strong enough to prevent us from backsliding. Every time the Pacific winds blew with gale-like convictions, our faith in the ship's stability was once again shaken to its foundations. The most vivid instance of my personal recanting occurred during a violent storm in which one of the signalmen, whom I considered "a cool number," became convinced that the 911 was about to capsize. Holding his emotions in check until he could no longer restrain himself, he broke the silence on the bridge that night with: "Mr. Kehl, do we jump clear the next time it rolls right?" At first I thought he was jesting, but a glance at his eyes revealed that his question was not intended to evoke laughter. Taken by surprise, I advised him to "hold it," but I wasn't at all certain that the next roll was not going to be the ship's last. Of course, it wasn't; the 911 rolled many more times before the storm subsided, after which my fair-weather faith was restored.

On that fateful trip from Norfolk that defined the endurance needed to survive, we discovered that seasickness was the standard condition—as much a part of amphibious life as bow doors, flat bottoms, and beachings. In retrospect, I have concluded that the sufferers could be categorized according to three major stages; fish-feeders, dry-heavers, and old sea dogs, with a few special or atypical cases. As a result of the preliminary screening provided by the Norfolk to Key West run, the crew consisted of two old sea dogs, two specials, and fifty-five fish-feeders.

Only Captain Smarba and the steward's mate, Frederick Jackson, qualified for old sea dog status from the outset. No one completely escaped; in psychobabble, the violent sea brought behavior modification to us all, but these two resisted more effectively than the others.   As the ship rolled more radically, the captain became noticeably less talkative; that was the only positive result of rough weather that I can recall, but despite his own quick adaptation to the ocean's turbulence, he was sympathetic and never said anything derogatory about the lingering fish-feeding status that gripped many of us.   Jackson likewise adjusted quickly; aside from the large sweat beads that dotted his forehead, he registered no outward ill effects.   Only two conditions could cause him to perspire profusely: a storm at sea or an excess of alcohol in his system; the difference was readily distinguishable because only the latter caused him to smile a lot.

Personally I was grateful that Jackson was relatively immune to the pain that an angry sea engenders. In a sense he took care of me during typhoons; the only food that I could eat without a fifty-fifty chance of seeing it again was applesauce, and over the three to five days that a typhoon raged before blowing itself out, I relied on Jackson to keep a supply of applesauce handy.

Of our two special cases of seasickness, one could be described as pathetic and the other as classic motion sickness. The pitiful individual was a young, muscular deckhand, large in both body and mouth. On the trip north from Charleston, he battled the physical effects of the sea with the same negative results as the others, but on the return trip around Hatteras, he simply lost his resolve to fight, groaned in his bunk for three days without moving, and refused any kind of assistance.

At the end of that period, the captain ordered me to get him on deck where the fresh air might revitalize him. To move this 200-pounder up a ladder to the open deck above without his cooperation required strapping him onto a litter so that four men could carry him.   The crew wasn't happy at such prospects because they were disgusted with his behavior; his unwillingness to exert any effort to cope with the same elements we all had to endure was interpreted as goldbricking or indulgence in self-pity.

On the assumption that they might have been justified in that assessment, I resorted to the water test prior to calling for the litter. I hit him squarely in the face with a pitcher of the icy cold stuff in the hope that he would spring to his feet in a rage. The experiment failed; he still didn't move. The incident was enough to convince the captain that this was one expendable sailor. Transferred off at Key West, he was reassigned to his native Brooklyn, where he spent the remainder of the war working in the local Navy yard, living at home, and enjoying his mother's cooking.

To all the guys who challenged the weather and refused to surrender no matter what the physical discomfort, this seemed unfair. But so is life. Certainly our yeoman, Chuck Waggon, could empathize with that sentiment. As I reflect on his symptoms, he suffered continuously from seasickness—from queasiness or even nausea—caused by the normal motion anytime the ship was underway, in both calm and thundering seas. The condition was so severe that, behind his back, he was known as Upchuck Waggon.

Wearing cotton ear plugs, Chuck flawlessly carried out his duties as long as the sea remained tranquil, but in stormy weather, he anguished in pain. After almost every storm, the yeoman urged the captain to transfer him ashore. His arguments, as meritorious as any, were always denied. Perhaps Smarba, because of his ingrained self-serving attitude, was unwilling to sign off on such a proficient worker. Although he was the only one in a position to provide an equitable answer to Chuck's problem, others of us should have interceded, even if it were a foregone conclusion that it would arouse Smarba's ire. In a combination of jest and frustration, Waggon once threatened to report the captain to Chicago's Mayor Kelly, whom he considered all-powerful in any realm, including the Navy.

Most of us, with no one to whom we could refer our concerns, advanced (if indeed *advanced* is the proper term) from the fish-feeding stage to dry-heavers. This apparently was a necessary stop before reaching the old sea dog plateau. One member of the black gang (engineers) just could not reach the dry-heaves hurdle. In rough seas he carried a bucket over his arm as he checked gauges and read meters throughout his four-hour watches. Determined to conquer the seasickness, he never complained, but others feared that his health would break if he continued to take the punishment. When the captain ordered his transfer to shore duty, he cried because he wanted to remain with the friends he had made aboard the 911 despite the threat to his health.

The dry-heaves stage was physical torture; the body retches but nothing is ejected. If an examination in later years had revealed that I had lost a kidney, lung, or two tonsils, I would have known immediately that the loss came during my months in the Pacific; the dry-heaves creates the sensation that everything inside has already gone. Making only modest strides through this stage, I felt that fate had dealt my progress a series of foul blows; every time the weather turned nasty, the crew that appeared on my watch seemed to include the most demonstrably seasick. I was okay until one of them began feeding the fish; then my system felt compelled to imitate him, even when I couldn't.

We all learned that the two most comfortable positions during a storm were on watch (out in the air) or lying flat in our bunks. Sailors would often go off watch, undress on deck, tuck their clothes under an arm, dash down two levels, and hope to hit their bunks before seasickness set in. The sea was so rough that, when they arrived, they had to tie themselves in with straps across the upper and lower parts of their bodies to prevent being tossed out by the ship's snap roll. The officers' bunks were constructed differently; I could keep from being tossed about by wedging a leg between the mattress and the top rail around the bunk.

I can vividly recall lying in that position where my eyes could not escape the lettering on the pipes that traversed the compartment near the bulkhead and just below the overhead. On LSMs all exposed pipes were labeled (e.g., diesel fuel, fresh water, salt water), but the stencil used to identify the diesel fuel was in error. Diesel was spelled d-e-i-s-e-l, not only above my bunk, but also at approximately fifty locations throughout the ship. Having seen that blunder several thousand times, it became an ingrained image that proved difficult to erase; I must still hesitate before writing the word to make certain that I am spelling it correctly. I venture to add that the same stencil compounded the same mistake on all fifty pipes of each of the more than one hundred LSMs commissioned at Charleston. Thus a reader who encounters a male in the three score and ten age-range who can't spell "diesel" may want to reflect on the possibility that he is confronting a LSMer.

Topside undressings followed by mad dashes to empty bunks were not uncommon in our struggle to combat the sea. Unconventional actions were necessary because in 1945 five typhoons struck the Okinawan area alone. Four of them, plus several other major storms, caught the 911 at sea. Fortunately our ship was safely ensconced in Subic Bay when the fifth and most powerful in the series hit the northern Pacific, causing some units to end up broadside on the beach while others dragged anchor or lost their anchors completely—frequently colliding with each other. Although not a part of this spectacle, we did experience fifty to sixty-five foot waves breaking across our bow while seventy to ninety mile per hour winds whirled overhead. Going to and from the bridge under these conditions was a perilous venture that necessitated gripping the railing with both hands to prevent being tossed overboard by the winds.

Because of its flat bottom, an LSM lacked the power to cut through the waves; the alternative was to ride up each succeeding wave, with the bow actually rising out of the water until the ship lost its balance and slapped with a thud into the trough only to be picked up by the next wave. This procedure, repeated every couple of minutes with uninterrupted monotony until the storm abated, was accompanied by two distinct sounds: the splat of the flat bottom hitting the water after the ship lost its balance and the roar of the engines as the propellers spun free for the brief period that they were out of the water as the ship took a header into the next trough.

Any attempt by an LSM to knife through the waves would have spelled doom. In a typhoon even a much larger vessel was no match for the sea; forced into such a challenge, the cruiser *Pittsburgh* was threatened with disaster; a 100-foot section of its bow was sheared off. When calm returned, another ship sighted this section floating in the China Sea where it constituted a navigational hazard. Aware of this floating danger, that captain was able to secure a tow line to it and, in a clever moment, radioed his superior to report the accomplishment. His message read: "Sighted suburb of *Pittsburgh*; took same in tow." When we reached Guam, that "suburb" was lying on the dock, a graphic reminder that, rough as it was to ride, the LSM was a survivor, a sea-going cork that was not about to be sliced in half like less storm-proof vessels.

CHAPTER 3

In Charge But Out of Control

Charged with overall operation, the captain of a Navy ship is assigned only one other responsibility; that of morale officer. In this second role, Captain Lester Smarba of the LSM 911 was an overwhelming success for a series of unflattering reasons. Just as there is no more compelling explanation for a feuding family to submerge its internal bickering than interference from the outside, so there is no stronger bond uniting a crew and its officers than a common foe—in our case, the captain.

His antics provided the cement that brought us all together. All four officers who served under Smarba respected each other, were dedicated to the tasks at hand, and were committed to cooperating with each other and with the crew in carrying out assigned duties. Eager to adopt the same spirit toward the captain, they were repeatedly rebuffed and gradually learned to push back.

The crew was a wholesome cross-section of American manhood. Reflecting after fifty years on its composition, I am amazed and gratified that we inexperienced officers were dealt such a dedicated and talented group that ranged from men in their twenties and thirties with superior abilities down to teenagers quick to learn and eager to confront the challenges of Navy life. To be trapped aboard our 203-foot sea-going cork for weeks at a time without major incident was a tribute to the crew's willingness to work harmoniously under the strains of war. Perhaps they overlooked the foibles of us officers because it was so easy to concentrate on the captain, a man who seemed to deserve all the criticism heaped on him because his behavior made him the bogyman in controversial situations.

A by-the-book officer, Smarba was eager to demonstrate, especially to review panels, that he could apply the book. After the 911 had been in commission for about a month, he realized that no one had as yet committed a Navy infraction warranting an appearance before a Captain's Mast, the lowest level of Navy courts. Smarba smartly concluded that we had to punish someone for something. To us officers he declared: "Let's put somebody on report. We can't have another inspecting team come aboard and find our Mast book still without any entries." Hardly an enlightened approach to discipline or an inspiration to a ship's morale, this attitude revealed his self-centeredness; showing that he knew how to record punishment became a coveted goal.

Always yearning for plaudits from above, the captain punctiliously obeyed all orders issued by anyone with a half stripe more than he had. At the same time, he concluded that anyone (especially his own four officers) with less rank than his could only provide an inferior point of view. His attitude toward the latter was not apparent to us at first, but gradually it penetrated our consciousness. No matter what comment an officer on the bridge made to him during mooring or docking operations, it seemed that he would do the reverse just to demonstrate how wrong his junior officer really was. If the officer suggested backing on the starboard engine, he would invariably order: "Starboard ahead one-third."

To verify our suspicions that he would always act counter to our recommendations, the one who happened to be on the bridge would watch the situation closely, study the captain's expressions, and when he thought that the captain was about to order "Port back one-third," he would blurt out: "Don't you think you should back the port engine, captain?" Almost always the captain would respond: "Port ahead one-third." Thus the best way to make certain that the captain would screw up was to provide him with the proper answers.

Impatient to the point of being churlish, he once asked me: "How long will that paint job take?" I hesitated momentarily with my answer so that it would be as accurate as possible. Before I spoke, he quipped, "That's too long," and walked away; but despite that behavior, he was an officer who clearly understood the techniques and advantages of keeping the 911 shipshape. Every inspecting team that came aboard, both stateside and in the combat zone, applauded our state of readiness. Even after several invasions, a reviewing group acknowledged ours as the best maintained LSM in the fleet; nothing was in disrepair, and all guns and equipment were ready for action. Smarba's uncanny ability to direct his officers in overseeing this maintenance was compromised by his administrative style; he couldn't convey his intelligent orders without making us dislike him, and his unwise decisions, when coupled with his lack of finesse, were ludicrous.

His maladjustment consisted of a mix of ego inflation, self-gratification, and an inferiority complex that was too broad to measure with a yardstick. Smarba suspected that the crew, his officers, personnel on other ships, and his Navy superiors were all conspiring against him. As a defense he was constantly plotting to take advantage of others; and when his machinations failed, he concluded that the other party, always conceived as the adversary, did him in. When there was no one available to bruise his ego, he adopted a do-it-yourself approach.

On learning that the LSM 911 was going to transport Army troops to the invasion of Luzon (Lingayen Gulf), he thought that we should engage the Army officers who would be aboard, in a friendly game of cards. After all, he contended, they had a lot of money, and we should relieve them of the burden of carrying it ashore. Not being a card player, I excused myself from the scheme, but Smarba felt that the Army officers should be enticed into a low stakes game at first, and if they proved inept, the ante should be raised in proportion to their demonstrated incompetence. As it turned out, they were better players than our officers, so the captain quickly aborted the plan to grub a few bucks on the side.

The three Army officers were genuine hometown boys committed to the jobs they were assigned. Living aboard for six weeks, they had no access to laundry facilities other than what we might provide, and the captain thoughtfully proposed that our steward's mate take care of their laundry needs. The service was gratefully accepted and carried out; the topic never came up again until the morning of the invasion. Minutes before we were scheduled to hit the beach in the largest landing attempted in the Pacific war to that date, the captain asked me to leave my battle station and report to the bridge "on the double" for what I assumed to be a crucial comment about the invasion.

Our crew was already at general quarters, and the Army had tested the engines of their vehicles and placed live ammunition in all of their guns; within a short time the Army personnel were to put their lives on the line and fight their way ashore. As I reached the bridge, the captain posed his vital question: "Did you make those Army officers pay for their laundry?" To my affirmative response, he added: "How much did you charge?" "The same as we pay, captain; seventy-five cents per week."

"It should have been a dollar. You know better than that. Those Army guys don't appreciate a thing. We have to get all out of them that we can."

Months later the captain gave another vivid demonstration of what he meant by getting all that was possible from others. When we were ordered alongside an ammunition ship in high seas to replenish our ammo supply, Smarba wanted to preserve our mooring lines (hawsers) that had dwindled in number and deteriorated in condition. Long periods of going alongside ships in rough weather had caused our lines to part and fray; replacements were not available, and our need was becoming critical.

The captain explained this plight to the other ship and asked if it would use its lines on this occasion; normally the ship coming in for the landing provides the mooring lines, and we were asking for a reversal in that procedure. The ammo vessel agreed to the request, but its deckhands, unhappy with this switch, provided a change of their own; they passed us the bitter end of the line, not the one with the eye in it as was customary. This particular line was exceedingly long (approx. 300-325 ft.), and our sailors had to tug and pull most of it aboard in order to secure it around the ship's bitts.

The captain drooled from the bridge as he looked down on all that excess hawser stretched out on our deck. Our regular mooring lines were about 125-150 feet long, and this one was more than twice that length. Because we were going to be tied up there overnight, the captain could not pass up an unethical opportunity to augment our hawser supply. Taking personal charge of his clandestine scheme, he called boatswain Spike Spangle to the wardroom, instructed him to take two sailors out on deck after dark, cut off 125 feet of the ammo ship's line, and bind up the end so that the tampering could not be detected.

Late that evening, the boatswain reported back that the maneuver had been completed without a hitch. That success caused the captain's brain to work overtime. He reasoned that, because the moored ship (ours in this case) normally supplied the mooring line, it was possible to steal the second half as well. If the ammo ship sent out a different deck gang in the morning, they might not realize that the line used the night before was theirs and would, in typical fashion, cast it off when we departed.

This too was cleverly executed. When we were ready to leave, our boatswain simply yelled: "Cast it off, buddy," and the ship's deckhand obliged; through chicanery we became the possessors of two hawsers that did not belong to us. The captain was so elated with his genius that he literally bounced around the bridge as we moved out to anchor in another part of the harbor, but this little larceny did not go completely undetected.

That afternoon an officer from the ammo ship came alongside and asked to speak with the captain. He was escorted to the wardroom where he explained that, by some unwitting mistake, we appeared to have acquired a hawser belonging to his ship, and he wanted it returned. The captain feigned shock and dismay that anyone in his crew would stoop to the level of heisting another ship's line, particularly at a time when supplies were critically low. He sent for the boatswain to come to the wardroom and asked him if it were remotely possible that someone aboard the 911 could have been guilty of such a despicable deed. The boatswain played it cool and asked for permission to go and check. He returned with the regrettable news that we did indeed have an extra line.

The captain berated him before the visiting officer and commanded him to get that hawser and place it in the visitor's boat. The officer thanked the captain for his prompt and forthright cooperation and left the wardroom just in front of the boatswain. As Spangle went out, Smarba whispered in his ear: "Be sure to give him only half." That was done, and the officer roared away in his motor launch unaware that his mission was only partially successful. A dejected captain watched from the deck and exclaimed: "Those greedy ships always look out for themselves; they come and take our line." The most incredulous part of this charade was that the captain believed he had been outmaneuvered and brooded over *his loss* because the ammunition ship had salvaged half of its line.

On another occasion, he had an opportunity to illustrate his attitude toward both his senior officers and toward us. When the 911 was ordered alongside an aircraft carrier to unload its empty shell casings, the seas were so choppy that it was practically impossible to moor an LSM to another vessel. All four officers advised the captain to request a delay in carrying out the order because of the weather. We believed not only that the task was dangerous, but also that senior officers with primarily big-ship experience possessed little knowledge of the limited maneuverability of a shallow-draft ship like ours in a heavy sea. He ignored our advice with the comment, "They have more stripes than I do," which to our civilian minds meant nothing in contrast to the evidence concerning flat-bottomed ships.

Smarba pulled the 911 alongside the carrier as ordered, but he quickly learned that he could not retain control because of the high waves. The ships collided and banged together time after time, until finally our mast was caught under the gun sponsons situated beneath the carrier's flight deck. The two remained tangled and battered by the sea for more than a minute with glass from the yardarm lights and pieces of metal raining down onto the deck. By the time the two ships were separated, the mast of the 911 was bent forward almost forty-five degrees out of position.

The mission was aborted, and the captain of the carrier sent us a message: "Sorry that you can't come alongside"—a fact that we had unsuccessfully attempted to get across to Smarba before he started the maneuver. Over the next few weeks before we were repaired, when sailors on other ships observed our appearance, they would ask: "Kamikaze?" In embarrassment, our crew nodded affirmatively.

Captain Smarba was no less dedicated or patriotic than anyone aboard, with all the abilities necessary to fulfill the duties of a commanding officer (CO). He ably handled the responsibilities inherent in his appointment, but could not cope with the power. A major part of his difficulty was personality, but part of it also can be traced to his earlier Navy experiences, which he never assimilated properly.

Commissioned an ensign in the Naval Reserve before Pearl Harbor and assigned to active duty, he encountered regular officers with little vision that war and the Navy's accompanying expansion would occur. As a result they were not particularly hospitable to reserves like Smarba in their midst. Snobbery

34

provides a partial explanation for their attitude, but according to Smarba's own statements, his irrational conduct was the real culprit.

On many ships larger than the 911, such as the one to which Smarba first reported, the officers were given a subsistence allowance from which to purchase food and operate their own dining facility separate from the ship's commissary. As a junior officer, Smarba was not assigned one of the more critical posts, but was placed in charge of the officers' mess, where he proceeded to create a mess of his own.

To add a touch of elegance to shipboard dining, his first major purchase was new wardroom silverware that he charged to the food fund, an expense that depleted the account. Faced with this NSF condition, Smarba was forced to levy an additional assessment on all officers so that they might have their "three squares" a day and thereby escape the embarrassment of only dawdling with their expensive silver service in the absence of food.

Because it tugged at their wallets in unaccustomed ways, this added outlay did not endear Smarba to his fellow officers, and his captain took special exception to Smarba's conduct when the latter accidentally discharged his .45 caliber pistol through the overhead and into the captain's sea-cabin. This spelled trouble "big time" for Smarba, because his captain confined him to the ship until he could break down, re-assemble, and identify by name the individual parts of his .45.

Consciously or otherwise, Smarba decided to inflict some of his former captain's techniques on us. Our reaction was that we had neither overspent nor shot off anything other than our mouths, but were confronted with attitudes and actions similar to those he had experienced. He failed to realize that, with the advent of war, Navy reservists, civilians at heart, now far outnumbered the regulars, particularly in the amphibious force; with fifty-three enlisted and five officer volunteers, plus one regular Navy gunner's mate, our complement was typical.

Despite the overwhelmingly cooperative attitude of reservists, it was impossible to indoctrinate this vast number of civilians who were inducted into the Navy with all its established traditions and nuances. Some flexibility on both sides was essential to allow the regulars and reserves to function as a unit. Smarba failed to grasp the delicate but radical shift that occurred between his previous service and his assignment to the 911. A major war was underway, and regulars and reserves had no choice other than to cooperate in the face of heavy reliance on the latter for manpower. Failure to comprehend these changes contributed to his frustration.

An early example of his officious character occurred when one of the officers overslept and reported late to the bridge for his watch. Although this was a one-time slip, Smarba ordered him to write out the duties of a watch officer ten times as a punishment. That was a humiliating and inappropriate conduct, similar in character to having to become intimate with the nomenclature of a .45.

In an equally unwarranted situation, he threatened to discipline me for refusing what I considered an outrageous order. After Smarba had run the ship aground and then successfully worked it free from the reef, he feared that the ship's seaworthiness had been impaired and directed me to send a sailor down to assess the damage, if any. Surprised by his request, I asked: "What will we use for diving gear? We don't have any aboard." I was even more aghast at the reply: "Use a gas mask. If it will keep out gas, it'll keep out water." Knowing that the two operated on totally different principles, I replied that I would not ask anyone to undertake an impossible (I meant

36

idiotic) assignment. We jawed over that one for several minutes before the engineering officer stepped in to inform the captain that his request was unthinkable.

Later, en route to the Okinawa invasion, Smarba again jumped me about what I considered a picayune offense. On the eve of our arrival in the Ryukyus, the LSM 911 was part of a hundred-ship convoy, totally blacked out, observing radio silence, and moving into position for the next morning. Understandably everyone was a little jittery. I had the midwatch when the captain came excitedly to the bridge. "Mr. Kehl, Mr. Kehl, what's that light on the port horizon?"

"Since there is no land in that area, captain, and since only a hospital ship would travel lighted, I presume that it's a hospital ship passing the convoy." Not expecting that answer, he replied in a nasty tone: "You're not big enough to decide if that's a hospital ship. I will decide if that's a hospital ship." After a brief pause, he continued: "That's a hospital ship."

Then he proceeded to berate me for not reporting the light when first detected. My defense was that the light was clearly visible and, if I saw it, the task force commander and his staff also saw it. The 911 could not change course or speed and specifically could not open fire without orders from the commander (unless in a dire emergency). Even if the whole imperial navy of Japan were closing in, we were not free to act independently. In my judgment, no purpose could have been served by notifying the captain, as I certainly would have done if we had been proceeding alone. It may have been a technical error on my part, but in my mind his conduct was another example of overreaction.

Each of the officers developed his own set of explanations for being on a different wavelength from the captain. Of course, I remember most vividly the incidents that vexed me, plus those that we experienced in common. Some of the most humorous and petty took place around the wardroom table, where Smarba gave some of his best performances.

Not content to be the autocrat of the breakfast table alone, he presided over noon and evening meals in the same iron-fisted manner—decreeing that the officers must sit at the table according to rank, with the executive officer at his right hand. Because there were only five of us, that seemed too formal to me, but before we had much time to complain about it, he added a second dictum: Tardiness at mealtime would not be tolerated (meaning that we must sit down when he did, regardless of the circumstances, or miss the meal). I can't recall any incident in which we gave him an opportunity to apply his late rule, but we toyed with it.

All four of us had difficulty making the breakfast deadline of 7:20. The steward's mate, per orders from the captain, was to awaken all officers at 7:00, but each of us seemed to wait for someone else to make the first move toward the head, with the result that we couldn't all wash our faces and comb our hair before the appointed hour for breakfast. With the captain's rule on punctuality, some of us, or at times all of us, had a choice: face and hair or breakfast. No one ever opted out of breakfast.

Part of the problem was that we had only one officers' head (washstand, shower, and commode), and the captain forbade us to use the crew's facilities. The other part of the difficulty was the captain himself. We were all too trusting and naive to suspect that he was engaged in an end run, but one day the steward's mate, feeling sorry for us, drew a verbal diagram of what was happening. We thought that through our collective inertia we had created our own problem.

Now it was a relief to know that the captain had tossed us a curve. According to the steward's mate, Smarba had quietly told him: "Wake the officers at seven, but wake me five minutes earlier." For days, even weeks, we never woke up to the fact that we were being blind-sided. Even if we had all leaped from our sacks promptly at 7:00, the captain would already have staked out the head. Generally he took most or all of the time before 7:20 washing, shaving, and combing his hair, if not washing it. That left us with the choice of breakfast or the head.

Without uttering a word of complaint to the captain, we decided to retaliate. One of us would get up at 6:50, and the other three would lie in our bunks until 7:20 and then get up for breakfast. Instructions to the early riser were that he must stay in the head until approximately 7:20 even if he had to sit on the john and read. That way the captain had a choice of face and hair or delay breakfast. Each of us took turns being the early riser and believed that four repetitions would convey the proper message without confrontation with the captain. On the fifth day, we returned to the normal schedule of rising at 7:00, hoping that our show of displeasure had modified the captain's special privilege. To our dismay, Smarba returned to his old routine of monopolizing all the time prior to 7:20.

That called for a grand finale. All four of us dressed and went to the head in advance of the captain's 6:55 wake up call; three of us stood in the shower with the curtain pulled. When the captain opened the door at his accustomed hour, he found one of us standing before the washstand methodically washing his hands and face. He slammed the door and walked over to a door leading onto the tank deck, looked at the sky, and waited until he heard the individual leave. Hearing the door slam, he hurried over and opened it, only to discover that another one of us was washing his hands; so he turned and gazed out the doorway at the great blue yonder until he again heard the door slam. When he attempted to enter, he again encountered another one of us standing before the washstand. We repeated the procedure until all of us had emerged singly from behind the shower curtain; in addition, the episode was so timed that the fourth walked down the companion way at 7:20.

Although never mentioned at the breakfast table, the maneuver rang an unexpected bell. The incident had apparently caused the captain to doubt his ability to concentrate and to react. He thought that there was a lapse of time between his hearing the door slam and an officer exit on the one hand and his walking over to turn the knob; he assumed that another officer walked into the head in those intervals. His look of wonderment was a sight to behold.

Smarba even took charge of our reading habits, an activity that constituted a major part of our enjoyment when not attending to the ship's operation. Although the 911 possessed a small collection of books, our reading consisted primarily of contemporary publications. The ship subscribed to three copies of various magazines: one for the forward crew's compartment, one for the crew's midship quarters, and one for the officers.

Mail, including magazines, came in spurts, depending on how frequently the ship moved from port to port. When the magazines arrived, the captain monopolized all of the officers' copies until he had read them. We never understood his motivation but advanced several theories: (a) he was insensitively selfish, (b) he didn't want his officers to know anything before he had a chance to read about it and was conceited enough to believe that the magazines provided such a monopoly, and (c) he assumed that as captain he had the right of first refusal and refused none.

Perhaps feeling a twinge of conscience to make the journals available to us within a reasonable period, he resorted to a crash reading schedule and occasionally brought two magazines to the breakfast table, placing one on each side of his plate so that he could digest and ingest simultaneously. The exec once laughingly commented: "He's the greediest guy in the world, the only man who ever tried to read two magazines while at the same time eating breakfast."

The exec's uncharacteristic outburst was the result of a particularly vexing morning. While the rest of us listened, the captain carried on a one-person conversation with himself. Leafing the pages of *Life* magazine on his left, he was fascinated by one page, held it up so we could all see, and exclaimed: "Look at the skimpy bathing suit on that one. Too bad they put one on her at all."

Then, turning abruptly to the eggs on his plate, he remarked to me: "Kehl, these eggs are cold. You're going to have to do something about those cooks." Before I could answer, his attention was directed to an issue of *Popular Mechanics* at his right elbow, which contained a disturbing article. "V-2 rockets! those damned Germans," he blurted out, "Why can't we invent something first?" After another assessment of the food, "The coffee's cold," his monologue took him back to the pages of *Life* to begin the animated reading cycle anew.

He demonstrated saner moments, but they too were tinged with an element of the unreal. Several times he came to the bridge at night during my watch and reflected on his postwar career alternatives. I gained the impression that I was basically a soundingboard for his random thoughts, which swept across a

41

wide spectrum of possibilities. One option was to return home to San Francisco where his father, a widower, lived alone. Lester's only brother had been killed in the European war, and understandably the father was anxious to have his only remaining family move close by. The father invited him to enter the men's clothing business as his employee, but Lester realized that the elder Smarba could not afford to pay him as high a salary as he commanded in the Navy. Because his position would be that of an apprentice, he was reluctant to accept that invitation although it provided a stable base.

His second possibility was to put down roots in Miami where his wife lived and where he identified two viable options. He considered opening a posh bar that catered to vacationers because, as he said: "Those shanty Irish flock in from Chicago. Someone's going to take their money, and it might as well be me." Then his mind jumped to a totally different idea; he could open a house of ill repute. "No one needs to know, not even my wife. I could have a swanky office downtown, pose as a commercial consultant, display a set of encyclopedias in the reception area, and spread a few trade journals around the office."

Both of these alternatives stood in sharp contrast to another idea expressed within ten minutes of the others. He could go back to school, earn a degree in education, and instruct the youth of America. Like his Navy career, something was out of focus concerning his future as well.

The Crew's Stew

The crew registered a thumb's down verdict on the captain long before the officers did. Their ire was aroused over an incident in which the captain ironically was thoroughly justified in his actions. Reid Mohr, the original executive officer who trained with the crew and who was the most popular man aboard the ship, had been a big-time college basketball star whose image was enhanced by having been to sea aboard a patrol craft in the Atlantic.

To a crew of landlubbers, his credentials profiled a natural leader. He took charge of recreation activities, mustered the Catholic sailors for Mass on Sundays when we were in port, and brought a relaxed attitude toward the challenges of war. Anyone with a problem or a special request consulted the exec and believed that he would receive the most sympathetic hearing possible.

In the structure of LSM duties, the executive officer doubled as the navigator. But on the shakedown cruise from Charleston to Norfolk, Reid Mohr demonstrated the limitations of the hasty wartime training he had received; he was incapable of determining the position of a ship at sea. When the captain asked how he had handled a previous patrol assignment along the eastern seaboard, Mohr replied with a smile: "Well, captain, when we got lost we just headed due west; when we sighted land, we went up and down along the coast until we spotted something familiar."

Smarba was understandably shocked. Because I had been exposed to navigation instruction more recently than any of the other officers, he assigned me to teach Mohr celestial navigation. Not the ideal teacher in this situation, I had no practical experience and had held a sextant in my hands only twice. Yet identifying the navigational stars visible in a particular sector was simple, and determining the position of three or more at a specific second was only a mathematical equation. My affable but distracted pupil was incapable of mastering these tasks; he realized this himself and reported to Smarba that these calculations were out of his league.

The captain reacted in the only responsible way he could: by asking the naval base to relieve Mohr and supply the 911 with a replacement. The crew was unaware, however, that their favorite officer lacked navigational talents and assumed that Smarba had replaced him because of a personal dislike. They pouted long over Mohr's departure, and the captain pouted because the crew pouted.

Within a few days, the Navy defused the crisis by sending us a competent and mature new exec, one of the most astute, modest, and firm gentlemen I ever met. In time the captain and the crew joined the other officers in recognizing him as a truly capable leader, but the crew never again fully trusted the captain. After a few months of festering, the situation reached the stage where any string of profane expletives, no matter how incoherent, denoted the captain.

Convinced that he had made the proper decision on Mohr, the captain was slow to forgive the crew's attitude. He became so suspicious that he thought they had deliberately goofed up several of the final training exercises at Norfolk and was determined to have retribution. That occasion came when the Navy decided to remove the two 20 millimeter guns at the bow and replace them with a single 40 millimeter.

The ship was assigned ten days of availability to make this and other alterations, meaning ten days in drydock that signaled an unexpected leave opportunity for the ship's crew. It created the ideal conditions for granting furloughs or at least seventy-one hour passes, but the captain announced to the officers that he would entertain no suggestion for furloughs or passes.

Being inexperienced and still naive, I accepted the captain's fiat as law. Within minutes the other officers had conceived a plan to counter his declaration, which served as my introduction to what nimble minds could do in the face of apparent defeat. Their plan, lifted from an elementary psychology text, was flawlessly executed within one hour. Witnessing that success, I became more daring in my own initiatives throughout the remainder of my career, both naval and civilian. I also realized that I was working in cooperation with three good minds and had to show some creativity in order to contribute to this struggle against a captain who seemed insensitive and unbending.

At the time, the LSM 911 was moored alongside the 912, which had been commissioned on the same day. Even before that, the two crews had known and competed with each other in their amphibious training at Little Creek; they had engaged in maneuvers at sea together and now were going into drydock together to have the same alteration in armament. The plan developed by my fellow officers to change the captain's mind utilized the presence of our sister ship. Nonchalantly one of our officers crossed onto the deck of the 912 and remarked to the executive officer: "Smarba has just authorized seventy-one-hour passes for the whole crew once we are in drydock." Taking the bait, the exec reported to his captain that we were authorizing passes. Not to be embarrassed, Captain Palmer of the 912 immediately announced that his crew would receive similar leaves. Our officers at once passed that information to Smarba: "Captain, we agree with your decision. The crew isn't entitled to any leave, but the 912 has just awarded seventy-one-hour passes to everyone. After all that these two crews have been through together, can we afford to appear any less generous than the 912?"

After screwing up his face a few times and mumbling several oaths, he agreed that nothing less would be politic; seventy-one-hour passes for all hands were proclaimed before the crew even knew what evil lurked in the captain's mind. At the same time I learned a significant lesson on how to manipulate the facts and redesign the truth.

Although not privy to the details of this maneuver, the crew was confronted with numerous opportunities on which to judge their leader. One incident that I recall vividly occurred during a midwatch while the 911 was underway in the South Pacific. I was on the bridge but was not rigidly enforcing a dictum issued when the ship had been commissioned. Smarba had designated the port chair on the bridge as the captain's chair, not to be defiled by any other occupant. I fully accepted and respected the principle that the captain should have a specific place to sit anytime he was on the bridge or was likely to appear, but at 2:00 AM when I was the officer-of-the-deck, I didn't mind if a signalman or the petty officer of the watch reclined in the port chair; I even did it myself occasionally.

On this particular morning, everyone was attending to his duties, with the signalman ensconced in the captain's chair, when Smarba, moccasins and all, came unnoticed up the ladder at the back of the bridge. He could have made his presence known simply by clearing his throat or by shuffling his feet. Either would have served as an adequate cue for the occupant to vacate his chair or for me to ask that it be done, but the captain wasn't seeking a simple welcome.

Annoyed that I had permitted the rule infraction, he elected to sound off with the classic child-like whine: "Mr. Kehl, someone's sitting in my chair." No Hollywood talent ever brought more pathos to those words. Although his rendition was heard only by the six of us on the bridge, by noon the next day, sailors throughout the ship were burlesquing the remark with "You're sitting in my chair" every time they passed someone who was relaxing.

The captain obviously was his own worst enemy. If we had been psychologists, we would have known that he suffered from the chronic need for AA (attitude adjustment). Although we were painfully aware of the symptoms, no one capsuled his condition succinctly until we had an MD aboard for a few weeks. After assessing the apparent differences that the officers were having with Smarba, the medic offered his professional diagnosis: He suffers from constipation of the mind and diarrhea of the mouth. That sounded appropriate at the time, but it didn't help much with a solution. Thus the captain's duel with all hands continued until he was transferred.

The 911, sporting bent mast, after collision with a carrier.

CHAPTER 4

Only One Oar In the Water

With a group as large as the crew of the 911, statistical possibility held that at least one member would hear the beat of a different drummer, but Hooligan, I fear, didn't hear any drummer. Not malicious, deceitful, antisocial, or surly, and certainly not ambitious, he was just there, probably because he had to be somewhere; and during the war, the Navy was a popular place to call home. He moved perceptibly in no direction until prodded, and then the starter generally rued his decision and agonized over the fact that he had been responsible for the push because, when activated, Hooligan became an accident in search of a place to happen.

I'm not sure I ever heard his given name, because the officers always addressed crew members by their surnames, and his fellow sailors were quick to dub him Happy. He was unorthodox even before his arrival aboard the 911, and he departed unreformed. Most of the crew had trained as a unit at the Amphibious Base in Little Creek, Virginia, while they waited for the LSM 911 to be commissioned. Happy was a late arrival, joining the team direct from the Navy brig at Norfolk.

He had enlisted in the Navy in 1942, endured the trauma of having the boot camp barber clip the flowing waves of black from his head, and vowed never to permit a re-shearing. When his hair grew and the barber beckoned a second time, Happy said adios to the Navy, wandered aimlessly off, and was declared AWOL for almost a year. After traveling halfway across the country, he stopped where he did for the practical reason that he was tired of moving. There his patriotic instincts caused him to take a job in a defense plant. When co-workers began asking about his draft status, he explained that he was 4-F. Suspecting that he was not believed, he packed up and retraced his steps several hundred miles and tried his hand at construction work, but that required more energy than he chose to exert. Strangely disappointed that the Navy had not tracked him down and discontented with life on the homefront for a single male who was a fugitive, he returned to Norfolk and surrendered voluntarily to Navy authorities.

Sentenced to eleven months in the brig, the equivalent of his foray back into civilian life, he was ordered to be placed aboard the first ship going to sea after his brig time expired. The LSM 911 was that first ship, and Hooligan had the distinction of reporting with a shore patrol escort; he arrived happy and affable with all of a sailor's normal gear, plus a pair of roller skates. While on his unsanctioned Navy leave, he had taken up roller skating for relaxation, and his skates survived the stint in the brig. Guarded as his prize possession, they contributed to his woes, because an LSM provided no readily accessible storage space for such items, and he insisted that they be close at hand for use every time liberty sounded.

Because most of the specific shipboard duties were already assigned before Happy's unique arrival and because sailors generally did not opt for mess cook duties, someone had to be appointed. That duty became his almost by default. It required him to aid the cooks in the galley, to serve the food at mealtime to one of the three crew tables situated a level below the galley, and to wash trays, silverware, and other utensils after every meal. Without any objection, he accepted this responsibility, from which he could be rotated after three months. In fact, he elected a second term because it provided him with more free time (in port, mess cooks enjoy liberty twice as often as other sailors) for his roller skating while we remained in the continental U.S. He even appropriated storage space for his skates in the locker reserved for trays, condiments, cups, and silverware.

Shortly after his arrival, the base sprung a surprise inspection on us, and the officer-in-charge asked to check Hooligan's serving locker for cleanliness and sanitary conditions. Prominently displayed inside an open door were the shining wheels of his skates, lodged between a stack of trays and a drawer containing knives and forks. The young inspector was elated, and the captain infuriated, that the former found something wrong. Hooligan was told in no uncertain terms to remove the skates. He answered, "Yes, sir," but no one gave him any guidance as to where they might be properly stowed.

It was always a mistake to permit Happy to rely on his own ingenuity, as he demonstrated on this occasion. The next time I saw the skates, they were in the freezer with a ton and a half of meat and other frozen foods. When I objected, he agreed to take my advice "to get them the hell out of there." I did not want to know where he concealed them next, because he considered the crew's storage space too inaccessible and any other location was likely to be unacceptable if detected. Several months later, I found them in the potato bin—camouflaged among the potatoes; no one could ever accuse him of not being ingenuous in inventing storage space.

As a mess cook, Hooligan was not popular either with me as the commissary officer or with the crew he served. He simply refused to put his mind in gear before starting his hands, legs, or mouth; after such a beginning, he always wanted to explain that whatever happened was someone else's fault. When he peeled potatoes, he invariably threw the paring knife away with the skins. His lapses were so regular that we could calculate how many times he had been on that detail by how many knives were missing. When the number reached seventeen, I threatened to put a hole in the knife handle and attach it to a string that he would be required to wear around his neck.

One day as I walked through the galley, Hooligan was waving a cleaver as though he were directing a band. Instinctively, I knew that something was about to go wrong. I asked what he thought he was doing but was not prepared for the reply although I should have expected the bizarre.

Reporting that the cook had ordered him to defrost the freezer, he was going to use the cleaver to chip the ice off the coils. Visualizing our full allotment of frozen meat about to be lost, I demanded that he "drop that damned thing immediately and never touch it again as long as you are aboard this ship." Because I was always prodding him to work, he was chagrined that I was preventing him from carrying out an order. The cook intervened with a few choice words about the principle of refrigeration, but Happy was unhappy. He wanted to blame the cook for neglecting to tell him at the outset that a cleaver was hazardous to the life of refrigerator coils.

The table for which Hooligan was responsible was in the crew's midship quarters, just outside the wardroom. Even with the door closed, I could tell how he and the crew were relating to each other at mealtime. After a few weeks I could read the language of noise. If I heard the trays being banged around, it meant that Hooligan was tardy in getting the food down; some were anxious because they were hungry, and others were eager to eat so that they could relieve the watch at the designated time. If there was a constant hubbub, it was the signal that the food was cold; if all was serene, it generally implied that someone had replaced Hooligan for the day.

He was accused of reporting that seconds were unavailable when, in fact, they were and of refusing to fill the coffee pitcher with the excuse that there was none in the galley. The sailors did not know when he was being truthful and suspected that he seldom was. They warned him, sometimes good-naturedly, of what was going to happen when his "cushy" job ended and he had to join the deck force. His general retort was that he was a far superior deckhand to all the others and that his talents were being wasted in the galley. From his storehouse of naval knowledge, he once offered the boatswain advice on deck painting, pointing out that it was far more efficient to pour the paint on the deck and spread it around than to brush it the old-fashioned way.

He believed that he could hold his own with any sailor. On the first day of his reassignment to the deck crew, the boatswain told Happy to grab a brush and a can of paint and select his own section of bulkhead. Other sailors were each painting sections of their own, and Hooligan attacked the assignment vigorously in an effort to justify his bravado over the previous months by endeavoring to complete his section first. To the amazement of all, he was the winner in time, but there was that one inevitable flaw: Happy had used a different color of paint than everyone else. Of course, he had an explanation: Someone had set him up with the different paint, a possibility I'll admit, but I was also convinced that if anything could go wrong, Hooligan would make certain that it did.

As a sailor on regular duty, he took his turn standing watch on the bridge. On numerous occasions when he turned up on my watch, he failed to see objects on the horizon that should have been reported. When questioned, he always had an excuse; he either thought that another lookout had already detected them even if they were clearly in his sector, or he would say something even more stupid such as, "I didn't think that that was important." One time when he appeared to be looking intently in the direction of a ship that came over the horizon, he said nothing. I waved my hand in front of his face and was startled to receive no reaction; his eyes were open, but he was standing there asleep—no mean feat.

Because Hooligan couldn't impress me, he tried to impress the captain and failed in every effort. One time the captain came to the bridge when I had the conn, looked at the receptacle for cigarette butts, and complained that no one had emptied it for days. Before I could say or do anything, Hooligan picked up the overflowing container and emptied it over the side. Again he made a little miscalculation; he had failed to check the wind, and all the ashes and butts blew back in the captain's face. He uttered a few oaths and took off. Hooligan asked: "How was I to know?"

On a second attempt to prove his seamanship, Happy again became a strike-out victim. He was standing with a boatswain and several other sailors at the starboard bow as the 911 was maneuvering to moor alongside another ship. As a preliminary to getting the heavy mooring line to such a ship, it was customary to attach it to a lighter heaving line, not unlike a clothes line; the end to be tossed contained a monkeyfist (a wrapped piece of lead) to make it easier to throw farther and to direct more accurately. Sailors pride themselves in their heaving-line prowess.

While our ship was at the outer limits of where a monkeyfist could reach the other ship, Hooligan begged for the privilege to throw and was told that he could try to toss it over. Making certain that he had the captain's eye, he took a professional wind-up and gave a mighty toss that easily reached the other ship; but as always there was a problem: Happy had failed to secure the other end to the mooring line or to anything else. Thus our heaving line was lost; both ends came to rest on the deck of the other ship where the sailors on deck roared with laughter, and our boatswain had to hurry and have another sailor do the job correctly. As the loose end flew gracefully through the air, the captain gave me a look of disbelief and shook his head. Typically Happy was as amazed as anyone and declared that he had been tricked; someone had untied the end of the heaving line.

Even in clothing, Happy styled his own. Shorts were not a part of any official Navy uniform, but, in the heat of the South Pacific, rules were bent; at first several sailors cut off their dungarees in an effort to keep cool; others soon followed the pattern, with shorts becoming commonplace, but many sailors made no effort to hem them. Strings on some hung halfway between the knee and the deck.

The captain ignored the rule about shorts, but issued an order that he did not want to see any hanging strings, "Irish pennants." He meant that he wanted all shorts to be hemmed, but Happy, always alert to new ways to frustrate officers and shortcircuit work, introduced a novel approach. Instead of hemming his, he stapled them. After one look, the captain was furious and asked what I planned to do about it. My reply was: "Nothing. By the time he sits down several times or after he washes them once, I think he'll get the point without any comment. The style isn't likely to become popular." I don't recall if the incident had any official ending, but it did not become a fad.

When it was announced to the crew at lunchtime that we would cross the equator that afternoon, Happy's curiosity was unnaturally piqued. I was scheduled to be on the bridge at the time of this rare event, and Happy, although not on duty, asked if he could come to the bridge to observe. I was pleased by his interest and encouraged him.

Because our geographical position was accurately computed at noon, I could determine the exact minute that we would cross the equator. At that time, I checked my watch and told him: "You are now a shellback." He looked aghast, asking with his eyes, how could that be? Apparently he expected to see a line of demarcation as shown in his grade school geography book or at least feel a little bump as we passed from one hemisphere to the other. After all, crossing the equator is far more dramatic than driving from one county to another at home; a slight bump in the roadway can often be detected where the resurfacing of one county ends and the next begins. In his literal mind, it made sense to expect such an indicator here.

The first impulse when anything went wrong was to check on how Hooligan could be involved. When we were passing through the Surigao Straits en route to the Lingayen Gulf invasion, the pressure began to mount. The Japanese had discovered our presence; we needed no internal excitement to stir the adrenalin. The convoy was spread out for miles; a group of landing ships, flanked by escort vessels, was followed, after an interval of three miles, by a horizontal line of carriers; after another similar interval, we were part of a second group of landing ships.

One night the first kamikaze I ever saw was shot out of the air off our port quarter; the next morning a carrier was hit and amid bellows of smoke was ordered out of convoy to cope with its fires. As we passed by, I felt that, except for the grace of God, the 911 could have been left behind to handle its own problems. But I hadn't considered the powers of Happy Hooligan, who quickly gained center stage by developing acute appendicitis; now we received similar orders to pull out of the convoy.

Having no doctor aboard, we had to ask the OTC for instructions. He ordered us and an LST with a medical staff to leave the group so that a doctor could come aboard (via rowboat in the China Sea) to perform the necessary operation. The other ships passed us by, and it seemed that we were on our own at the mercy of kamikazes as late afternoon and evening approached; sunrise and sunset appeared to be the favorite times for such planes to come out of a low sun to attack. The attitude that Happy had done it again was more prevalent among the crew than was sympathy for his misfortune. There seemed to be no situation that he couldn't screw up.

We had to improvise an operating table. The doctor recommended the crew's dining table located at the bottom of the ladder leading up to sickbay, and it was cleared for action (sugar bowl and salt and pepper shakers removed). Assisted by our pharmacist mate, a mortician in civilian life, the doctor went about his task as though he daily rowed to the office and plucked out an appendix.

The captain thought that he should be hospitable and invite the doctor to stay for supper. I was commissioned to extend the invitation and watched part of the operation before finding an appropriate time to interrupt his cutting and suturing. I wasn't sure that the doctor should be bothered but finally popped my question. Without looking up, he asked what was on the menu. I didn't feel the least bit sick until I began reciting foods, but then the view of the bloody excision got to me. The doctor thought for a minute and concluded that the fare on the LST that evening was more tempting, stitched up Happy, placed him on the bunk at the foot of the ladder leading up to sickbay, and rowed off.

The 911 and the LST rejoined the convoy before dark and experienced no further excitement until we hit the beach at Lingayen where Happy challenged the Japanese for our attention. From sunrise that morning, the ship was at general quarters; that meant no one was in or out of the compartment where Happy was recuperating. Before and during the initial stages of the landing, the battleship *California* bombarded the coast. The roar of guns reverberated throughout the ship, but no one was around for hours to apprise the patient of conditions on the battlefront. That was indeed an oversight. He panicked, left his bunk, tried to climb the ladder to see if the ship was still afloat, fell, and broke his stitches. Under those circumstances the pharmacist mate recommended transferring him to a hospital ship where he could receive the care necessary to prevent infection.

Like MacArthur he returned. Back aboard in a month and slightly subdued, he remained throughout the war. Shortly after the Japanese surrender, the Navy issued a point system for discharging personnel: one point for each month of service and an additional point for each month of sea duty, plus points for individual honors; at the outset, the point total necessary for a return to civilian life was high and was then gradually reduced. This readily became the primary topic of conversation; individuals were comparing notes on who would be leaving first and who would be going together.

Hooligan did not fit into such discussions. His was a special problem. In time, he came to confide in me and sought my advice concerning the negative points he had accumulated. Having been AWOL and in the brig for a total of twenty-two months, he received minus points for those months and still had a minus eight when the war ended. Thus he owed the Navy months of service before he could start accumulating points toward discharge.

Aside from this obstacle in becoming a civilian again, Happy wrestled with a second problem. During his AWOL jobs before he gave up and returned to the Navy, he banked money under the two fictitious names he assumed when he had worked as a civilian. He wanted to know how he might best reclaim his deposits. With only common sense as a guide, I advised him to withdraw the money under the aliases he used to deposit it. I had no answer to any bank request for identification that he might be asked to present, but legitimately the funds were his under any name. Not being around for the conclusion of the Happy saga, I cannot report on his subsequent exploits. According to my calculation, Happy was scheduled for discharge sometime before the Korean War, unless he screwed up again.

There Were Others Too

Happy wasn't stupid—just a composite of a male Calamity Jane and an individualist who made a career of refusing to be on the same page with those around him. Not typical, he provided an unwelcome change of pace to the high-spirited and technically proficient crew that included appropriate quotas in all the various personality categories: sea-lawyers, pranksters, eager beavers, card sharks, poets, lover-boys, and whiners, plus several irreversible losers.

The most perverted prankster repeatedly conducted a simple biological experiment on his unsuspecting shipmates. He had read that, if a sleeper's finger(s) were immersed in water, lukewarm or a little hotter, the reaction would be an immediate and uncontrollable urge to urinate. Intent upon testing this hypothesis, our amateur "researcher" was constantly on the alert for a crew member asleep with a hand dangling over the side of his bunk.

When the wag found such favorable conditions, he would gently ease one or more of his would-be victim's fingers into a can of water at the appropriate temperature, hold the can there for fifteen seconds, then remove it, sneak off to a clandestine observation station, and await the reaction. If his subject moved slightly and groaned a lot in disbelief, the prankster accepted the sounds as evidence that he had brought forth a gusher. If the sleeper merely jumped from his sack and made a frantic dash for the head, the "researcher" concluded that the experiment had succeeded, but fallen short of perfection.

The king of the losers was equally aggressive, but always achieved negative results. Horace Borus, by his own confession, was studying to be a genius. Without a brain transplant, his goal was doomed from the outset, but he endeavored to give it the old college try without either college or high school certification.

By some means, Borus had acquired a one-volume encyclopedia that contained a blurb on the title page reading: "all the facts you'll ever need to know." A literal-minded Horace interpreted this to mean that, if he mastered the factual contents of this thick, odd-shaped (6" x 6") book, he would achieve genius status, an objective that far surpassed any claim made for the one hundred great-books-theory of knowledge. Because he equated memorizing with learning, he set out to commit the mountains of facts contained in that one tome to memory. After he thought his brain had been permanently impregnated with a few facts, he would ask another member of the crew to test him with certain questions.

One afternoon as I was walking through the crew's quarters, I interrupted such a test in progress. It concerned the capitals of the forty-eight states. The tester, who wasn't much brighter than the would-be genius, seemed impressed by what could be learned by studious application to a text. He thought that it would be fun if I competed with Horace and proposed that we take turns identifying the capitals of states that he would name; the one who missed first was the loser. I obliged, and the contest came to a screeching halt when Horace couldn't decide whether Philadelphia or Pittsburgh was the capital of

61

Pennsylvania. As he deliberated, he declared that any fool should know which of the two to select, and he was absolutely correct in that assessment.

The second topic under study that day was the presidents of the United States. Horace asked if I could recite them in order. When I asked if he preferred them forward from Washington or backward from the present, he knew that I was already on the road to genius-hood. I lacked the nerve to tell him that this was not learning. Believing that he could never comprehend the term *assimilation* and that memorizing was a harmless exercise, I didn't disrupt the pseudo-paradise he had carved out for himself.

Borus became the victim of every scam in a sailor's repertoire—even an order that sent him to the engine room to obtain a quart of green oil for the starboard light. When he returned with the explanation that it was still on order, he was sent back to get "some regular oil" for the electric light in the radio shack, but he didn't need someone to trick him into demonstrating his gullibility; he was fully capable of performing nonsense unabetted. Once he endeavored to prevent the Navy day from dawning by tying the master-at-arms in his bunk while he slept. Horace reasoned that, if no one wakened the crew in the morning, night would continue, and everyone could sleep in. Unfortunately his scheme backfired when he tied up the petty officer who didn't have the duty that morning. He frankly admitted: "Dis ain't my day."

With this kind of astuteness, he was potential prey for a card sharpie, especially after he had sold his collection of silver dollars for seventy-five cents each. Where Borus was concerned, I feared that he could lose his monthly pay to a fast shuffle; at least while his nose was buried in the genius-book, that was not going to happen.

Of course, I did not come to appreciate fully all of the shipboard personalities like Horace, but because of my role as Commissary and Stores officer, I did establish a close rapport with the storekeeper, Oliver Wendell Wisor. A competent petty officer, described as a social flake, he introduced himself to the crew by his full name. They expressed the hope that they would not have to spit out that complete handle every time they addressed him. He was agreeable: "No, just call me Sammy." "Why Sammy?" was a much more logical question than the answer: "Because that's my father's name."

Unwilling to accept that nonsensical remark as a bona fide reason to call him Sammy, the crew, after a few trial balloons, concluded that Budd was an appropriate moniker. Henceforth he was labeled Budd Wisor, hardly a proper designation for a guy who, by his own confession, was addicted to coffee and once drank thirty-one cups in a day. He was the proverbial bundle of nerves, who considered coffee the best hope of maintaining a grip on reality, but naturally it handicapped his sleeping. As a result he would lie in his bunk at night while his muscles jumped for a few hours; then he would get up and return to the coffee routine. Although he looked dissipated, he was always able to perform well, but I was relieved that he wasn't called on to stand behind a 20 mm gun or read a radar screen.

In spite of his idiosyncrasies, Wisor contributed more to the morale of the ship than he probably realized. He and I worked together to try to satisfy the crew's preferences in food, in supplies, and above all in a desire for a payday at the end of every month. He loved to brag to the crew about what he had procured for them, and he always put the best face possible on our failures. This reflected favorably on me and the ship administration because it required no explanations on my part for what we failed to accomplish, and bounteous credit was extended for what we achieved.

A poignant example occurred in the South Pacific where the reefers established meat quotas. In order to requisition a ton of beef, an equal amount of Australian mutton had to be purchased. Personally I found the mutton tasty, but the crew was generally suspicious because it wasn't American. With one reefer I argued, although the claim was totally false, that we had been forced to accept all mutton at the previous supply base because there was no beef. Thus we should not be penalized and should now receive all beef and no mutton. The supply ship bought the argument, and Wisor reminded the crew when we were served steak that, if it hadn't been for that ploy, they would be eating the mutton they disliked.

On another occasion we found a way to outmaneuver the captain and provide the food the crew preferred. Without any previous hint of dissatisfaction, Smarba announced one day at lunch that he had eaten all the canned peaches he intended to consume in the foreseeable future and ordered me to requisition no more although the crew preferred peaches over all other canned fruit. This disregard for the majority represented a flareup of his selfish nature, plus a slavish addiction to a Navy dictum that required the officers and men of small ships to eat the same food daily. A simple change could have provided the captain with a substitute dessert every time the rest of us were served peaches; although that would have bent the rules slightly, it would have been eminently more equitable than forcing the whole ship to conform to the captain's whim.

For our next reprovisioning trip, I asked Wisor to type up requisitions for canned plums, pears, and fruit cocktail while eliminating peaches. When the captain signed the stack of requisitions, he specifically checked to see that peaches were omitted from the list. During our trip by motor launch to the supply ship, Wisor watched me draw a line through the plum and pear items and pencil in peaches. Before he could comment, I said: "Wasn't it too bad that they were out of pears and plums and had to substitute peaches. You see; it's right there on the requisition. Who can argue with that?" Although Wisor agreed with the sentiment, he questioned my disregard for the facts with "That's deception." I replied: "Deception, hell. If the crew doesn't receive the peaches they want when they are available, *that's* deception. We're promoting morale and preserving the captain's standing with the crew." The modified requisitions were honored, and to my knowledge, Wisor never revealed the facts to the crew, and I chalked one up against Smarba.

One of the most eagerly anticipated and rewarding times for members of the crew was payday, but the fact that the calendar proved that a month had passed did not mean that the eagle was about to scream. Because small ships did not have disbursing officers aboard, the 911 was at the mercy of base supply officers for their pay. All of those men had day-to-day duties of their own, and handling the payroll of small ships was a secondary responsibility, one that they were often clever in dodging, sometimes justifiably.

The most common tactic, aside from outright refusal, was to agree to such a request with a week or ten-day delay, hoping that the ship would receive orders to sail in the meantime. Admittedly a ship's payroll entailed considerable work; after the pay records were delivered to the office, each account had to be reviewed and computed for amounts assigned to dependents, war bonds, clothing, promotions, and possible changes in all these categories since the last pay period.

After a few rebuffs from disbursing officers, I evolved an offensive strategy that generally produced the desired results, and Budd let the crew know that it frequently required some conniving to make payday possible. When I called on a disbursing officer and received one of his excuses, I never argued or attempted to cajole him; I simply said: "Please put that in writing so that, when I go to your commanding officer in search of an alternative, he will know that I already talked to you and was apprised of your excessive workload." Not wanting the issue carried to his superior, the supply officer generally found a way to sneak our payday into his routine.

Once I ran into a supply officer who was genuinely overwhelmed with work. He was not perturbed that I threatened to go to his commanding officer even after I poured out the sad poverty tale that our sailors were in dire need of all types of clothing and urgently wanted their hard-earned cash to make essential purchases.

That was more truthful than one might suspect. After the U.S. Army had been in the Philippines for a short time and paid the Filipinos to work for them, the locals had relatively large sums of money and no place to spend it. Our sailors arranged to relieve them of their funds by selling their personal belongings. The natives were eager for any cloth they could get their hands on, and the sailors' skivvy shirts, work shirts, and dungarees, plus rags, all of which sold at exorbitant prices, were the most readily available.

Until this time, the supply of rags used in the engine room and the bilges seemed limitless, but after a few calls in Philippine ports, the pile began to dwindle, even after we requisitioned a second ton. It became necessary to declare the void where the rags were stored to be off-limits to all except motor macs, because the crew was selling the larger pieces to the natives. As a major result of this enterprise, our men were not broke, but there was an urgent need to replenish their wardrobes. I didn't consider it propitious to provide the details of our clothing crisis to the disbursing officer and dwelt on the poverty theme.

This overworked officer sympathized with my stated plight but apologetically concluded: "I can't help you, even if you go to my commander, but I understand your predicament. I do have access to clothing (shoes, shirts, and skivvy shirts) and can arrange to have them delivered to your ship free of charge this afternoon." I felt that I had played out the string as far as I could and accepted the "freebies"; more than a hundred pairs of shoes (assorted sizes) and hundreds of various types of shirts were dumped on the deck as promised. The sailors had fun rummaging through the gifts to find the proper fits and temporarily forgot that payday was overdue. Wisor was elated at what he thought was a coup, but I wasn't certain; I feared that it might lead to a new round of sales to the Filipinos. Of course, Wisor explained to the crew how this manna had ended up on our deck.

At the outset of his career on the 911, Budd Wisor had found it a little difficult to understand my priorities. Because the ship was small, with little storage space as Happy Hooligan's roller skates demonstrated, I did not want to bring any non-essentials aboard. While we were still in the States, the cooks recommended that we purchase five yards of muslin to be cut into filters for the coffeemaker. In order to be safe, I modified that to ten yards and had Budd prepare the requisition accordingly.

When he presented the request, the supply officer informed him that they only sold muslin in bolts. Thus Budd returned with much more than requested. While he was still coming up the ladder, I saw the bolt and yelled: "Wisor, how long do you expect this damn war to last? We will both be dead of old age before that bolt will be needed in the galley." When he declared, "That's the way they sell it," I was not overjoyed and asked with some agitation in my voice, "Do you work for me or for the base? When I want ten yards, tear off that amount and tell them for me that they can shove the remainder wherever they want."

Wisor thought he understood, but several weeks later he returned with another unwelcome item: two huge boxes of paper towels that we had not requisitioned. Before I could say anything, Budd rushed up the ladder and blurted out: "Mr. Kehl, they were free. I didn't even have to sign anything." Because the ship made no stated use of paper towels, I shot back: "I don't give a damn if they were free or if they paid you to take them. They were free because no one uses them. Where are we going to store them?" I don't know what happened to the towels and never asked. One night shortly thereafter, Wisor probably tossed them over the side, but those were the only disagreements, if they can be so defined, that we ever experienced.

On liberty Budd was a loner, but always reported having encountered beautiful women. I can't attest to their beauty but can vouch for the number he engaged long enough and seriously enough to obtain their names and addresses. Unfortunately for me, he felt obliged to write to each of them. I know because I was the censor who had to approve his mail. If we were in one place for five days, he generally had five addresses that translated into five additional letters. On one largely uneventful trip from Pearl Harbor to Funifuti (Ellice Islands), he wrote fifty-one letters that I had to read.

I tried to jest with him about his correspondence, pointing out that I obviously didn't keep him busy enough. I threatened that, if he persisted in flooding me with such a stack of mail, I would give him an assignment, any assignment to utilize his time, even if it meant opening every case of canned goods and recording the serial number of every can so that he would be too tired to write letters.

For the most part, his letters were babble. He presented these girls with wild accounts of confronting the enemy, with guns smoking, bullets flying, shrieks of pain from the enemy lines, and Navy gunboats churning all around him. I said to him: "Wisor, we haven't even seen a Jap. Why do you spread this melodramatic nonsense? Take pity on me; I have to read it to see that you are not saying something that is confidential, particularly when you simulate combat situations."

With a smile he replied: "I'm practicing my creative writing." With a "listen to this, fellas," Budd would convert all crew members in the compartment into a captive audience and proceed to read his most creative letter of the day aloud. At times he would lapse into bad poetry, none of which I can recall except for a little ditty that he sent to a girl in his hometown. "Oh how I wish again, to be back home again in dear old Michigan." When he knew that I was in the process of censoring the mail, he would occasionally knock on the wardroom door and ask if I had read a particular letter yet. Once I answered affirmatively, and he solicitously asked: "What do you think of that one, Mr. Kehl? Isn't it a wow?" Then he wanted a critique.

As I reflect on these episodes and incidents after a half century, I can only be nostalgic about the Budd Wisors, Happy Hooligans, Horace Boruses, and the fifty other personalities aboard the LSM 911. I would sincerely welcome an opportunity to know how their lives developed after the Navy experience. Although some registered no interest in assuming responsibility, many were only twenty years of age when the war ended.

Maturity and the GI Bill of Rights undoubtedly converted many to responsible pillars of society, but I am intrigued by some questions: Which ones? How was their stewardship recorded in the annals of time? Which ones were the major surprises? Did Budd Wisor continue his college program in hotel administration that was interrupted by the war? Did Hooligan ever accumulate enough points to be discharged or did the Navy grant him a special dispensation? To a person preoccupied with education and learning, it would be gratifying to spend several hours with each of these individuals, but the reality is that, with a few exceptions, I must be content with my reflections.

CHAPTER 5

Shipboard R & R

Adequate rest and relaxation, along with bitching, were concomitants of a happy ship. Landlubbers could always relieve tedium and tension by walking around the proverbial block, but that was not a luxury available to men aboard a 203-foot LSM. Within such constraints, sailors enjoyed few options to boredom and to each other's quirks. During our days at sea, the repertoire was limited to the basics of reading and writing, plus card-playing as a substitute for 'rithmetic. In port, especially in the States, sex, real or fabricated, added a whole new dimension, and no description of Navy liberty would be complete without its inclusion. For some, "a girl in every port" was an empty phrase, and they desired it that way because of the girl back home, but for others it was reality at its creative best.

At the outset, I must confess that much of my information on the sex life of LSM sailors is hearsay. Officially

I can report that no member of the 911's crew ever contracted VD, but some were at risk. According to Navy brochures posted on all ships, the VD rate among Filipino women was 130 per cent. That didn't daunt the actives who thought that statistics were something in a book. A few dismissed the assertion merely as a shock tactic, having learned at their sixth grade teacher's knee that 100 per cent was the saturation point; but they did not continue to read the smaller print explaining that some Filipinos were infected with two or three strains.

If sex can be interpreted as a humorous topic, such qualities were revealed during our stopover in Cebu City. A coterie of our sailors considered it hospitable to call at the local brothel where, after extensive examination, one sailor was rejected. Apparently all the girls looked him over and concluded that he was oversized. Although I had been aware that some clothing manufacturers charged more for merchandise that was labeled XL and XXL, my limited knowledge of the oldest profession never included any reference to size. None of the girls felt equipped to accommodate an XL, so they sent him out the door ungratified. His satisfied companions teased him unmercifully and laughed all the way back to the ship. The unfulfilled one arrived angry, frustrated, almost wild, and urgently in need of a cold shower.

The shipmate who reported the incident to me summed it up in a few words. "Y'know, he hung like a mule." Not having grown up in mule country and not having heard the expression before, I was forced to recall old *National Geographic* photos in order to fully appreciate this analogy. Then I too roared with laughter.

When we headed out to sea after any period of liberty in which everyone enjoyed being ashore two or three times, sailors on watch reported tales of conquest. Although nothing was addressed to me, I overheard these conversations, which were partly to brag to each other and partly to impress me. The more sexually oriented believed that they had a mission to convert as many as possible to their view of sex. Nothing was more cherished than accompanying a seventeen- or eighteen-year-old on his first call at a whorehouse.

Years later one of the sailors confided that a fellow crew member with money, the card shark of the outfit, connived to maneuver him to a brothel against his will. The instigator shelled out a reasonable number of greenbacks to a prostitute and told her that the amount would be doubled after she had enticed his companion into her lair. The sailor walked away, but the prostitute pursued him down the street, even taking him by the arm, before she finally accepted defeat.

Not always finding it necessary to go in search of sex, our men discovered that it sometimes came to them. When the 911 was anchored close to shore, Filipino women would row out to get acquainted. One night at dusk, I noticed a gathering of sailors at the stern, not a normal congregating spot, so I walked back to catch the attraction. A boat with five young women aboard was tethered by a frayed line held by one of our sailors; another was already in the boat. I ordered him back aboard and the boat to shove off, but I was not naive enough to assume that the boat with the aggressive, young prostitutes would not return once I had gone below. Either the sailor on watch ignored the situation or was distracted so that the extracurricular activity could be continued. In fact, one sailor actually went off "in a beautiful pea-green boat" with one of the women and didn't return for three days.

That AWOL jaunt came several weeks after V-J Day, and when he reestablished his connection with the Navy, he requested permission to be discharged in the islands so that he might marry the girl. During his absence from the ship, he lived in the family hut and had purportedly developed a rapport with the girl's father, who promised to make him a successful "cane farmer." Until I heard his glowing and positive description of hut life, I never understood what the phrase "poor white trash" meant, but at that moment, the pieces came together in my mind and he was the personification.

Previously I had been perplexed by his random talk in partial sentences that were often garbled so badly that it was difficult to grasp the meaning, particularly when his mouth moved and the words seemed to be emitted through his nose. Now his "trashy" talk and wild proposal of a native marriage based on a three-day grass-hut romance completed the picture. Fortunately the incident ended abruptly when the captain refused to comply with his wish, stating that the regulation permitting an overseas discharge was ill-defined and the procedure vague. That killed the issue; the sailor accepted his foiled marriage as though he had been denied a second piece of pie, remained aboard, and was decommissioned with the ship.

I can personally attest to the sexual aggressiveness of the Filipinos when an attempt was made to draw me into their net. One morning as I jumped off the ramp of the 911 and headed for a Navy installation ashore, I was suddenly joined by a ten-year old, barefoot Filipino pimp, running to keep up with me. He invited me to have sex with his mother for three dollars. Thinking that I had not heard him correctly, I kept walking without answering. On the assumption that I was mulling over his proposition, the kid repeated it. At that point I, advised him to get lost, whereupon he made his final pitch: "She ain't never had it before, mister." Ordered to take his huckstering elsewhere or I'd call the SPs, he got the message and moved on.

When I returned to the ship that morning, I was confronted with another aspect of the sex urge. We immediately loaded an Army cargo for Okinawa, and the ship was readied for departure. Just before the ramp was raised and the bow doors closed in preparation to retract from the beach, an excited Filipino came rushing up and asked to speak with an Army captain whom he called by name. Having not yet met the Army personnel who were scheduled to accompany the equipment, I asked him to wait while I went to the wardroom to check. I found Captain Clem Phlegm, who said that he would explain later but to tell the Filipino that he wasn't aboard. I did so and returned for his explanation.

Apparently the Army captain and the Filipino had made a deal, and the former was welshing on his part. About a week earlier, Phlegm had agreed to give the Filipino a large Army oil-burning lantern in exchange for the privilege of sleeping with his wife. The Filipino kept his part of the bargain, but the captain, never intending to surrender the lantern, feigned a use for it until he left the island and promised to deliver it at that time. He deliberately told the Filipino that he was leaving a day later than scheduled, but our preparation to sail immediately was obvious to everyone. The "local" was at the ramp to collect the lantern as his part of the immoral barter, but without knowing the details, I had turned him away.

Ironically clever Clem wasn't home free; perhaps the Filipino held the trump card. Either from the latter's wife or from another of his earlier escapades, Phlegm had contracted VD. From the first day at sea until he left the ship at Okinawa, our pharmacist's mate injected him daily with penicillin. Nonchalant about the affair, Clem simply assumed that it was our duty to provide the necessary treatment; after all, he was a fellow officer, but from our perspective, he proved to be the most ungrateful slimeball we encountered during all our work with the Army and Marines.

None of our officers, I am pleased to report, succumbed to this level of behavior, but neither were we totally immuned to the subject of sex.   With us it was strictly a topic of conversation, and the focal point was often a book entitled *Ideal Marriage* by Theodoor Van de Velde. What Dr. Spock's baby book was to infant care, *Ideal Marriage* was to sex. And one copy never served so many so well.

Not general issue, our copy had been purchased at Sears in Honolulu on our way to the Pacific front. Oblivious to the fact that we might be starved for reading material in our leisure hours, I accompanied Ben Dover on liberty one day when he suggested that we consider laying in a supply of books to pass the inevitable idle hours. I had never thought about that aspect of Navy life, but he proceeded to select a few volumes by H. Allen Smith, and I thought that I should follow his lead. As a budding historian, I discovered two recently published history volumes: Charles A. Beard's *America in Midpassage* and Bernard DeVoto's *The Year of Decision*. In our browsing, we came across *Ideal Marriage* as a change of pace from both Ben's choices and mine.

This intriguing title became an instant hit not only with the officers aboard the 911, but also with mere acquaintances. When ships would come alongside, officers often asked if we had any books that we were willing to trade. We told them about the Van de Velde volume but refused to surrender it permanently; we occasionally agreed to lend it to others who promised to mail it back after they had perused it. Their word was always kept, but sometimes it reached us from strange ships and unknown individuals because our borrowers passed it on to others who, in turn, dropped it in the mail to us. We can only speculate on the percentage of naval officers sexually educated through our inter-library loan program.

Any discussion of sex seemed always to lead to a difference of opinion. Although we were not about to admit it, the truth was that each of us realized that the others knew little about the subject, and we could blunt each other's arguments by aggressively asserting any vaguely plausible point no matter how unfounded in fact. We delighted in such freewheeling discussions, and when differences occurred (almost always) that the others would not accept, we consulted *Ideal Marriage* as our "sex bible" and then interpolated its passage to prove whatever we were arguing.

This volume's most memorable role in our repartee came after 8:00 PM one evening at Okinawa, during a two-week period in which the executive officer was recovering from an appendectomy aboard a hospital ship. Although we were at anchor, we kept a third of the ship's crew at battle stations because of the threat of an air attack. In the exec's absence, the captain volunteered to stand the eight to midnight watch. That afforded the other three officers not only a break, but also an opportunity to be alone in the wardroom for an extended period without Smarba's intervention because, without the captain's stint on the bridge, one of us would always have been on duty.

Brooding over a Navy decision, the gunnery/communications officer, Earl E. Byrd, had just come off the watch. To exacerbate his rare foul mood, Ben and I sympathized with his plight because we too shared his agony, but not in the same compelling way at that moment. When all three of us had been inducted to active duty, an ensign was being promoted to lieutenant (jg) after nine months in grade; promotions were contingent only on time served, and superior performance was not a factor. As the officer corps became top-heavy through previous advancements and direct commissions, the length of time in grade for all ranks was constantly being extended. For each of the last six months prior to that fateful evening of debauchery, Earl remained a month away from an apparent promotion because of the policy requiring extended time in grade. On that very day, the latest promotion list was released; individuals with his date of rank were still at least one month away.

Earl planned to take a shower before hitting the sack and in anger jerked open his underwear drawer with a little more gusto than usual. That rattled a fifth of whiskey stored behind his shorts and socks. We had each purchased several such bottles at Pearl Harbor on the advice of officers who had gone to the front ahead of us. "You may be glad to have it" was the admonition. Cheap and available, it presented no storage problem, so we, the untried in battle, fortified ourselves as recommended.

Until this particular night no one had "popped a cork," but Earl now became a popper. In his depressed state and alerted by the rattle in the drawer, he announced that he was about to drink to his non-promotion because of the interminable delays. Ben volunteered to sample the stuff once the seal was broken. I, on the other hand, never entertained such a thought; the red flag went up in my mind, not because of my limited experience with alcohol, but because I was scheduled to relieve the captain at midnight; I couldn't afford to appear on the bridge with liquor on my breath.

Torn between the need for four hours of sleep and a desire to be a part of the verbal festivities at least, I allowed my gregarious instincts to win out. Actually I had little choice; the chest of drawers containing the tongue lubricant was alongside my bunk in which I was already ensconced. Anxious to express my sentiments concerning an inconsiderate Navy that seemed intent on keeping us as ensigns for the remainder of our natural lives, I joined the "cocktail hour" that gave expansive meaning to the term. As frequently happened, the conversation drifted from the promotion list to sex. I can't recall how that came about, but several hours into our session, *Ideal Marriage* was invoked to settle a dispute between Earl and Ben. Because they had succeeded in reducing the fifth to a fiftieth and experienced difficulty not only in reading the passage, but also in turning the pages, I was relied upon to render a judgment based on my reading of the text.

Under normal circumstances, no one of us would have entrusted another to interpret passages from "the bible" for him. Now both were extending that power to me: proof positive that alcohol had submerged their real personalities. Being the only stone-sober one of the three, I realized that this was not a discussion I could take pleasure in controlling because Ben and Earl were both under the influence. After several failed attempts to break it off, I tried to withdraw, roll over, and get a few winks before reporting for duty.

That never happened; the boatswain's mate came through the door at 11:30 to awaken me (ha! ha!) so that I might relieve the captain. I dressed and headed for the bridge, knowing that at best the next four hours would be shear torture because of the lack of sleep; the possibility also existed that the calm might be disrupted by an inopportune air raid. Earl and Ben planned to resume their routines that had been interrupted by the presence of the fifth; despite his inebriated condition, the former was still determined to take his shower, and Ben prepared to hit the sack because he was scheduled to relieve me in four hours.

The aftermath of our bedside chat began to unfold when Ben came to the bridge at 3:50 AM. Before hastening down for some much needed rest, I asked if Earl had taken his shower without incident. "That was a damned mess," Ben reported. "When he didn't come down from the shower after a reasonable time, I went to check him out and discovered that he was still standing in the shower with his shorts and socks on. I finally got him to bed, but I feel like hell. That must have been lousy whiskey."

Bleary-eyed and exhausted, I quickly made friends with my mattress and heard nothing more about the night before until 7:30 AM, when Earl was preparing to relieve Ben. After describing how hung over he was, he proceeded to his post; I briefly considered substituting for him but dismissed the thought when I realized that my next turn on watch was coming up at noon.

When Ben came down, he reported how he had passed his four hours on the bridge. Despite the morning air, he was unable to shake the effects of his drinking bout. Shortly into the watch, he explained to the boatswain that he was ill and curled up on the deck of the bridge, wrapped his life jacket around his body, and tried to sleep it off.

He admitted that "several times the boatswain shook me to report flash red," a condition that required ships to send all hands to general quarters because an air attack was imminent. "I acknowledged the flash reds but told him I had confidence that those planes would never penetrate the screen and rolled over. What was I to do?" To defend his inaction further, Ben continued: "If I had sounded the alarm, Earl, in his state, would never have found the bridge" [his battle station]; with a smile he added: "and you would have yelled at me instead of the Japs for disrupting your sleep." It took several days for us to get rested, but that was the only time all of us did not give the Navy a 110 per cent effort.

Hearts & Spades

Leisure hours on cruise ships are supervised by recreation directors. The closest an LSM came to experiencing that luxury was a deck of cards. Those fifty-two little pasteboards kept many of us from boredom and possible early retirement to a rubber room.

Almost everyone aboard played cards in some form. Although ship's rules discouraged gambling to prevent animosities from developing, our naivete was not such that we assumed that no money changed hands; our intent was to confine it to reasonable limits. Fifty years later, I learned that our surveillance had not been as effective as supposed. Information revealed that we had at least one card pro aboard, the same one who tried to buy a prostitute for a recalcitrant fellow sailor. At one time he banked $2,500, rescued from the paychecks of his shipmates as a result of his card-playing skills: not bad for a high school dropout whose postwar ambition was to own a yellow Buick convertible. He obviously concluded early that he could separate more money from his petty officer superiors than he could ever earn from serious application to tasks that might lead to a promotion that, in turn, would bring a few extra dollars per month.

Apparently there was nothing underhanded about his winning; he was simply more skilled than his competition, but there was one devious, though hilarious, card-playing episode involving a less skilled player that I did experience without having to wait a half century to appreciate.

Max E. Padd was having such bad luck in a game of Hearts that he fit the adage: if his luck hadn't been bad, he wouldn't have had any luck at all. Players and bystanders attested to this phenomenal streak, and he exhibited increased irritation with each hand. As the game progressed, the ship was approaching a harbor, and Max predicted that he would draw a playable hand just when the order came to "Set the anchor detail" of which he was a member. With that remark, an inspiration dawned on several of his fun-loving friends: Why not secretly give Max a pat hand and simultaneously make believe the ship was about to anchor.

The details were quickly worked out. Max was deliberately called out of the compartment for a moment; in that interim the cards were arranged for him to receive a hand that would assure him all the tricks. One of the pranksters had already gone up the ladder until he could see across the deck and reported that the 911 was about to reach its anchorage. Also a signal was relayed to the wheelhouse where the P.A. system was located, and as Max returned and picked up his cards, a crackling noise came over the P.A., a recognizable prelude to an announcement.

After a pause, the voice began "Set" and another pause followed. With that Max slammed down the cards, uttered a few obscenities, and headed for his anchor detail station. Then the voice continued: "Set right where you are; we're still beyond the harbor mouth." With those words everyone in the compartment burst into laughter, and Max flew into a rage.

The captain, who had strict rules against using the P.A. for anything except official messages, was on the bridge at the time and faintly heard the sound that was designed to be heard inside the ship. Knowing that he had issued no order, he asked the officer-of-the-deck, who was alert to the prank, why the P.A. was on. Without hesitating a moment, he answered: "There's a glitch, and the electrician is testing it." A satisfactory response and end of caper.

Hearts was also the pastime that occupied most of the officers' leisure hours. As often as possible, we resorted to a friendly, no-money game, always playing with the same partners: Earl and Ben versus me and the exec. We arrived at this combination by happenstance. The captain had assigned us certain mealtime positions at the table, and from habit we always sat in those same chairs anytime we were at the table.

Methodically we kept a cumulative game score, not on paper, but in a more permanent but inconspicuous spot on the cross beam, hidden from view by the top of the drapery that separated the sleeping and dining sections of the wardroom. We could just flip down the top of the buckram-stiffened curtain with a flourish and record the result each time a game was completed; because of our seating locations in relation to the partition, Ben and I were the designated scorekeepers, each recording his team's victories. If anyone else ever stumbled on our unique scoreboard with all those lines in groups of five, he would never understand that he had uncovered the key to much of our social life for more than a year.

Hearts was new to me when I reported aboard, but my colleagues promptly explained the fundamentals. Each hand consisted of twenty-six points, one for each of the Hearts and thirteen for the Queen of Spades alone. The object was to stick the opposition with as many Hearts as possible and with the Queen, denoted as the "black bitch" in our table parlance, but if one team collected all twenty-six points, the other was assessed twenty-six points, a real coup in a game where the low score wins. Of course, if a team takes up the challenge to capture all twenty-six points and ends up with only twenty-five, the excitement level is raised. After I accomplished the feat of gaining all the points a few times, Ben good-naturedly remarked after one such success: "That's old cement-head. You tell him that it happens rarely, and he's trying to prove you wrong with every hand."

Today I haven't the slightest idea which team carried off the laurels at war's end, but my guess is that, after hundreds of games, the margin between the two was slim. Our marathon tournament was halted abruptly with the fall of Japan and the Navy's simultaneous decision to make radical personnel shifts. That combination broke up the "old gang," but Hearts proved to be our most enduring means of relaxation.

We did possess the ingenuity to invent an alternative to counter monotony. Labeled Pin-the-Tail-on-the-Captain, this was not a skill contest, but one that relieved a lot of tension. The most creative player in this regard was the engineering officer, Ben Dover, who designed and carried out two masterful strokes. Because the captain found it difficult to see us enjoying ourselves in our regular games of Hearts, he always found an excuse to disrupt the game by sending one of us on a mission anywhere outside the wardroom.

84

When he could devise nothing novel on the spur of the moment, he resorted to an old stand-by: complain that the temperature in the distiller was too high. That observation was a cue to activate the engineering officer because Smarba demanded that it be checked immediately. Of course, the temperature had to reach 212° to create steam to convert salt water into fresh water, but the captain didn't comprehend that; he would come into the wardroom and exclaim: "Mr. Dover, you'll have to do something about that steam; it's at 212° again. We don't want an explosion."

After he had been summoned away from a card game several times to check the "still," Ben decided to make a game of it. With Smarba unaware of what constituted steam, Ben would rush out every time the captain came over his refrain. In his haste to attend to the "faulty" equipment that was "about to explode," Ben would drop his cards on the deck, turn over a chair, or go out with only one shoe on. Slamming the door, he would stop, linger outside for a moment, and listen to determine if his theatrics had caused any of us to "crack up" in the presence of the captain.

Another of his games was intended as a deliberate payback for one of the captain's absurd requests. Ben explained to the other three officers that he was going to tell a non-joke at dinner that night, and he wanted us to laugh in an effort to test the captain and see how he would react. In the course of the evening meal, Ben looked directly across the table at me and asked: "Why is a duck?" When I responded "How should I know," he replied: "The higher it flies the much." Of course, this was total nonsense, but we all roared, including the captain. In an instant, he realized that there was no joke except the one on him. Because no one had addressed anything to him, he could not retaliate even though he suspected that he had been set up.

As I now reflect on it, this non-joke was difficult to surpass for meanness, but we tried. At times we found ourselves in a "top this" joke-telling mood, and the captain, who could never be confused with a wild and crazy guy, would attempt to join in. As far as we could tell, he knew only one joke and repeated it every time he thought his input was expected. It wasn't really funny, but he insisted on relating a make-believe conversation between a diner in a restaurant and a slightly tongue-tied waiter.

Diner: "What are these odd-shaped things in my soup?
        peas or beans?"
Waiter: "Kidley beans."
Diner: "What did you say?"
Waiter: "Kidley beans, sir."
Diner: "Oh, you mean kidney beans."
Waiter: "That's what I said, diddle t'I?"

We never understood why he thought this was funny, but if you are a no-joke guy, I guess, that's what you go with. When times were really dull and the captain was present, we would instigate a joke-telling session just to see if we could get him revved up enough to join the conversation by repeating his "kidley bean" story one more time.

In addition to group activities, each of us devised his own personal techniques to stave off boredom. When the 911 was underway in areas where it was safe to toss floating objects into the water, I at times decided to practice my marksmanship. After convincing someone to randomly throw cardboard boxes or gallon cans off the bow of the ship, I tried to hit them with my .45 pistol as they bobbed on the water past the stern, where

I was seated on one of the bitts. The exercise netted only demoralizing results; before the whole crew, I demonstrated that the Japanese had little to fear from me at close range.

Scoring on one out of ten of the floating targets, I decided to take up a less precise practice: namely, seashell collecting. This mindless endeavor consumed innumerable hours both when we were beached (while the Army or Marines unloaded their supplies or equipment) and when we spent endless hours at general quarters waiting for the appearance of enemy planes or for an "all clear." Being on the beach at low tide afforded an excellent opportunity to patrol for shells, and Okinawan waters were home to some of the more exotic specimens.

My cache was stored in a can of fresh water at the stern on a longitudinal at the corner of the potato bin and was brought out for processing every time we labored under a prolonged "flash red." I spent those hours meticulously picking sealife out of the shells with a safety pin or other sharp probe. The procedure produced fish-scented hands, but sitting idly by in the hot sun waiting for an elusive enemy wasn't my prescription for an idyllic afternoon either. As I picked and pushed at the shells, I envisioned them being converted to sparkling pins, bracelets, or earrings; none of those materialized, but after the war I did enlist a silversmith to mold a pair into a set of cuff links.

Variety to such idling activity was supplied by a "passenger" who was aboard for a brief three weeks and who advanced relaxation to an art form. Trained as a physician, he experienced twenty-four hours of leisure every day and was a candidate for boredom, but skillfully fought it off. When the Navy assigned him as a doctor to our LSM group, the commander realized that he had no quarters for him on the same ship with others on the flag staff. The 911 was happily selected as the beneficiary of that coincidence; Dr. P. D. Attrix fitted in well with our officers, joined the card-playing, answered our health and diet questions, and talked lovingly about his wife, Gerry Attrix. For some strange reason, we never approached him about our sex debates. Perhaps we were too embarrassed to confide, or preferred to let him think that we were sufficiently informed, or didn't want our lively discussions on the subject marred by the facts.

Compared with the rest of us, P.D. was a newcomer to the Philippines and learned quickly that he needed a hobby to fill the otherwise empty hours. Souvenir seeking was taken up as a logical choice. Any time we were on the beach, he went on a search. After one exploring expedition, he returned with what in my mind was a primitive, worthless hatchet; the blade and face appeared to have been hammered out in a local blacksmith's shop and fitted with a handle hewn from weathered hardwood without demonstrating any particular craftsmanship.

Seeing nothing special about the tool was a clear indication that I lacked P.D.' s creativity. When we were next at sea, he spent hours "restoring" his hatchet. After polishing both the wood and the blade, he prevailed upon a motormac to drill a quarter-inch hole in the end of the handle, induced a boatswain to provide a twenty-inch piece of marline (a loosely twisted white cord about the diameter of a common clothesline, used by the Navy to decorate stanchions and railings), died the marline with red ink supplied by the yeoman, ran the marline through the hole in the handle, and formed a tassel where the ends came together to complete a loop. With these steps, a fake artifact had been created.

By the time this physical labor was completed, he had conjured up a vaguely plausible yarn about the hatchet's prominence. Knowing that during their occupation the Japanese had forbidden the Filipinos to speak English, he wove this historic fact into his tale. According to his mythical chronicle, when a Filipino was caught violating this dictum about the "vulgar tongue," he was publicly reprimanded; the common form of punishment for this indiscretion was the amputation of a finger, a ritual in which a member of the local constabulary wielded Attrix's invention, the ceremonial hatchet, in the village marketplace to intimidate the locals against further use of English.

In contrast to our frequent beach appearances (called back repeatedly by popular demand), the battleship sailors seldom set foot on land. When we were moored alongside such ships, members of their crews were anxious to buy any souvenirs we were willing to sell, even at outrageous prices. P.D. Attrix spun his ceremonial hatchet tale for the big ship sailors and actually demonstrated how the Japanese administrators wrapped the red cord, a symbol of regal authority, around their wrists before inflicting the punishment.

His listeners were enthralled by the vividness of his rendition; it sounded as though he had witnessed at least one such mutilation. Without further inducement, they began bidding against each other for the right to purchase his two-dollar hatchet. When the ante reached $160, there was a pause, and then an officer asked: "Will you accept $200?" Unwilling to take advantage of this gullibility and desiring a graceful withdrawal, Doc explained that he had to decline all offers because this was a treasured artifact, and he considered it his duty to deliver it to a museum where it could be viewed by

Americans for years to come. That did not, however, end his gift for tall tales.

When Attrix examined a rusty-bladed, brass-handled dagger that I had picked up ashore, he began to weave a credible history for my acquisition. With a smile he launched out anew. "This is a relic from the period of the hated Spanish occupation of the islands and was worn on the belts of local marshals as a symbol of royal authority." After a pause, he continued: "You can take it from there; add to my introduction. I project that you have a $150 to $200 item, and I don't want a commission." His estimate may have been accurate, but the dagger never went on the market, is still in my collection, and serves as a pleasant reminder of the breath of fresh air that P.D. Attrix brought into our routine. I feel certain that the ceremonial hatchet was also retained by P.D. after he went home to become a nationally renowned surgeon.

A New Day

With the end of summer in 1945, the people of the world began to unwind and reflect on the meaning of the Allied victory. We aboard the 911 began to celebrate a little earlier. Captain Lester Smarba had received orders returning him to the States. "There was not one single crew member that I know of who wasn't deliriously happy," one of the sailors wrote to me forty-nine years later. "It was like Christmas, New Year's Day, birthdays, and graduations all rolled into one happy occasion."

Throughout Smarba's captaincy I was angered by his demeanor, as the sailor so aptly phrased it, but I never thought about its origin, even when it approached this sad ending. No one offered to assist him with his luggage as he struggled to get it off the ship at the time of his departure, and everyone was conspicuously absent so that no one would have to shake his hand as he left.

Now as I look back on his shipboard attitudes and actions, I begin to see the root causes; he and the crew had misinterpreted each other from the beginning. Most of the crew had spent all of their lives being instructed in elementary and secondary schools, in boot camp, and some in specialized Navy schools. This pattern was continued at the Little Creek Amphibious Training Base, where the captain and all of the crew except me and several enlisted men trained as a team for ten weeks under the tutelage of base personnel. Praise was handed out by the base staff as appropriate, and further instruction was provided as needed.

When they all reported aboard the 911, they expected to retain their quasi-student roles, with Smarba assuming the same kind of leadership and direction that had marked their lives to this point; after all, almost ninety-seven per cent were going to sea for the first time—and under war conditions. They needed direction, but Smarba definitely did not recognize this as his responsibility. Even if he had understood their need, he would have failed because he was not a teacher, despite his comprehensive knowledge of the Navy; he taught me most of what I learned in the service, but his abrasiveness was such that I resented him in the process.

He assumed that all enlisted men and the officers were already proficient in their duties and needed no further instruction. They, in turn, wanted praise when due and guidance when necessary to correct their mistakes. But he offered none. His displeasure when orders were not carried out promptly and correctly was publicly on display. As a result, the crew developed the idea that he had little respect for them as individuals, an attitude that was accentuated by his failure to speak to any of them when they passed each other in the companion way or were on the bridge at the same time.

With Smarba's departure, Earl E. Byrd became the new commanding officer, and I served as his exec. That combination was intact for only several weeks when Earl also was reassigned. I continued as second in command, but Dan Brady was transferred in as the new skipper. Dan's arrival was the last piece of evidence necessary to make it clear to all that a new day had dawned in the life of the 911.

His first and last address to the crew deviated widely from Navy standards; it left no doubt that all vestiges of the formal, doctrinaire, and at times picayune reign of Smarba were history. He explained his theory of administration in a few blunt and novel remarks:

> *I am happy, even pleased, to be here. Two inspection teams have already declared the 911 the cleanest and most battle-ready ship in the amphibious fleet. Obviously I didn't contribute to that, a ranking that cannot be improved upon, so consider me just a guy along for the ride. Ensign Kehl is in charge, and that's all you need to know. He can call on me and you can call on me if you think I can help. By the way, I like to read at night. If anyone has any good westerns, they're my favorites, I'd appreciate having them when you are finished. Carry on.*

Not prepared for this sudden switch, I found Dan's greeting to the crew unsettling and even scary because, with his brief comment, we were transformed from a spit-and-polish structure to one in which the captain became almost invisible.

With those pithy remarks, Dan set about to lead the life he had vaguely outlined. To begin his daily routine in port, he read westerns from around midnight to 4:00 AM, then slept until noon. Over the following hours, he showered and shaved, had brunch, read the mail, wrote to his wife, and was on his way to the Officers Club by three. Back to the ship by six, sometimes with several friends in tow, he was ready for the evening meal, to be followed by either a double feature movie or one movie and a few hands of cards before starting through his twenty-four-hour pattern again.

Dan always invited me to accompany him to the Officers Club and seemed genuinely disappointed when I declined. Such invitations stood in sharp contrast to the Smarba era, when no officer in more than thirteen months was ever invited anywhere socially by the captain. Dan, an incurable extrovert, was anxious to introduce me to his readily acquired friends as the man who ran the most ship-shape LSM in the Pacific. In all fairness, Smarba deserved much of the credit for that distinction, but Dan didn't worry about such details.

The movies that we watched at night by dropping a bed sheet for a screen from the 40 mm gun mount were the result of Dan's ingenuity. Some ships acquired projectors, but we were not so blessed; the captain, however, traded for one, but temporarily the deal seemed meaningless; the bulb to make it operable was burned out.

Always the optimist, Dan sent a boatswain to the supply depot for a replacement. When he reported back that projector bulbs were not a stocked item, he happened to mention that the supply terminal had a projector similar to ours for its own use. That caused a light to go on in Dan's opportunistic mind, and looking at me, he replied: "That's the answer. You and I will go to the base together and heist the one from their machine. You'll explain that you are looking for something else, say a sprocket for the reel. While you go into the stockroom with the clerk, I'll lag behind and remove the bulb from the projector on their table." There is always joy when a plan comes together as Dan's did. We finessed the bulb with ease, and it served our needs for the remainder of my tenure on the 911.

In those postwar days, neither Manila nor Subic Bay was an exciting liberty port. Thus the shipboard movies afforded an excellent alternative for evenings of relaxation. Personally I was attracted to one particular film. Entitled *Music for Millions*, starring Jimmy Durante and child-phenom Margaret O'Brien, it introduced (at least to me) June Allyson. Because I had never heard her name before and because she was not a headliner, I concluded that she was my personal discovery.

Having not seen an American woman in person or on the screen for more than a year, I knew at once that June Allyson was the most exquisite being ever to appear before my eyes, a feeling that lingered for years. Based on that assessment, I asked our projectionist if he would re-run the film; he consented, and with a handful of similarly afflicted sailors, I was enthralled a second time. Convinced that this was the all-American girl that men dream about, I decided that, when I reached the Los Angeles area, I would attempt to call and ask if she would have dinner with me. Dan's influence was obviously causing me to think more aggressively, but it didn't result in positive action. When I picked up a newspaper at Pearl Harbor some months later, I learned that June Allyson had married Dick Powell.

94

Dan Brady's presence not only provided a boost to everyone's morale, but also brightened my professional outlook. His approach meant much more to me than evenings of relaxation. During the Smarba years, none of the officers had ever anchored, moored, beached, or docked the ship; the exec and Byrd both became captains with no such experiences; but the first time we were underway in Dan's era, he turned to me and said: "It's all yours." We were in Manila harbor and ordered to go alongside another LSM to pick up half of its crew for liberty. Most of our men who also were going on liberty, as well as those on the other ship, lined the decks to observe my maiden mooring fiasco.

At first all seemed to be going well with my approach, except that I had not calculated the current properly; (the current in Manila Bay is one of the strongest in any harbor of the world). Without factoring in that one condition, I gave the proper calls to the engine room, but sailed completely past as though I had no intention of going alongside. Dan didn't take over, but ordered me to go around for a second approach. I improved but still did not slow the 911 sufficiently to get the mooring lines over. On the third try, although not a textbook maneuver, I succeeded in getting the liberty party aboard.

After that embarrassment, I received other opportunities to dock, moor, and anchor. In time I acquired a confidence that heretofore had been nonexistent and felt more like a well-rounded deck officer. In step with the crew, I truly hailed Dan's arrival as a breath of fresh air.

CHAPTER 6

Around the Table

"Now hear this: Chow down! Chow down!" Probably the most popular and eagerly awaited command ever bellowed over a ship's PA system, this message was rivaled in enthusiasm only by mail call or a captain's announcement that liberty was about to begin.

Response was always prompt and reactions lively. Not only an invitation to eat, this was a summons to socialize. For ships at sea, mess call was also a prelude to a change in the watch, a bristling, exciting time of day when at least two-thirds of a crew came together. Tradition held that this was a time reserved to sound off about the food; but in truth, our crew, comprised almost wholly of reservists, did not know that they were expected to appear unhappy with the meals they were served although they certainly realized that this wasn't the homefront.

Everyone in the 911's complement grew up during the Great Depression, and many were appreciative of the regularity of meals and the abundance of food in the Navy larder. Because the depression had not abated until the war in Europe stimulated our nation's economy, the tribulations of those lean years were still vivid in the memory of most young Americans when they entered the service where many pulled their feet under Navy tables. Although metal trays, dehydrated potatoes, and powdered milk registered graphic evidence that this was not mom's kitchen, these mealtime innovations thinly veiled the fact that many were eating food as wholesome as they ever had. I'm sure that no one could convince a sailor that the food was as good as he received at home; the simple fact was that mom wasn't there to cook his favorite meal, butter his toast, peel his orange, or provide other personal touches that account for much of his attitude concerning his Navy fare.

No one would confuse galley food with gourmet dining, but why prepare pheasant under glass when it had to be eaten from a metal tray? The cooks consistently turned out nutritious meals that frequently snubbed Navy tradition in the process. Influenced only by what we liked and what was available, civilian habits prevailed. Almost never did we have beans for breakfast, and the Navy staple, shit-on-a-shingle, seldom appeared on the weekly menu. What did appear was almost always in quantities sufficient to satisfy even the avaricious appetite.

In that atmosphere, one sailor attempted to eat his way into the Guinness record book by establishing a new plateau for pancake consumption. That particular morning, the 911 was scheduled to get underway before he topped off his pancake-eating feat. Assigned to the stern anchor detail, he took his position while clutching the final three pancakes in his hand. Not able to decipher from the bridge what this slender, diminutive guy was shoving into his face and certain that he was not chewing on his knuckles, the captain via the ship's phone system asked for an explanation.

Stern Talker: "It's his breakfast, sir; he's eating pancakes."

Captain: "Why is he still eating? Didn't he get to the table on time?

Stern Talker: "He was on time but just didn't get finished. He's trying to break a record."

Captain: (In a rare jovial mood) "Whose record?"

Stern Talker: "His own, sir."

Captain: "How many pancakes has he eaten?"

Stern Talker: "These are the last, numbers forty-one, forty-two, and forty-three."

Captain: "Why is he stopping now?"

Stern Talker: "The cooks ran out of batter."

Generally our sailors ate everything that was set before them; their most visible way of congratulating the cooks for their culinary artistry. But anytime we had Army personnel aboard, whether for a few days or for a month, the cooks received rave testimonials, both through words and actions. The great variety of hot food available won most of the accolades, but no Army group was more amazed than the hospital unit we carried to the Okinawan invasion. Almost in disbelief, they applauded the Navy's ability to follow its normal mealtime pattern despite the possibility that the war could roar overhead at any moment.

The landing took place on Easter morning, April 1. Our Army unit was not needed that day and remained aboard for all the meals. Since the regular Sunday menu called for chicken, no exception was made because we were in a war zone. To most of our passengers, it was an eerie sensation to be close enough to see their Army comrades taking command of the beaches but not close enough to disrupt the Navy routine. On this occasion, that meant a full hot dinner with metal tray, eaten to the sound of battle in the foreground.

Although the Army relished our food, they at one point developed a higher appreciation for our silverware. Just as we were about to land an Army unit in an area that had not yet been secured from the enemy, the cooks discovered that practically all of our silverware was missing, having been clandestinely appropriated by the Army. When this major pilfering job was reported to the captain, he announced over the P.A. system that the ship would not beach until the silverware was returned. He explained that cardboard boxes would be placed outside the two doors amidships, and when they were filled with approximately a hundred sets of knives, forks, and spoons, the Army would be permitted to exit.

Although he advised them that no retribution would be exacted from anyone involved in the heist, that carrot was not really necessary. One situation Army personnel wanted to avoid in time of an air attack was being aboard ship; with the realization that such was their destiny unless the silverware made an appearance, they readily recognized the error of their ways and coughed up the loot. Thus we were not forced to eat with our fingers until we reached the next supply ship.

The 911 was able to be so generous with its food to both its crew and its sometime passengers because of Navy allocation procedures. Funds were appropriated according to the size of a ship's complement: the smaller the complement the higher the allowance per individual served. Because an LSM was reasonably small, we received next to the highest per person allocation. The only exception occurred when passengers pushed up our numbers and thereby lowered our unit allowance.

Every three months, every ship was required to conduct an inventory and provide the Navy with a financial statement pertaining to food consumption. We had to show the actual cost of feeding all those for whom the 911 was responsible against an allowance formula established by the Navy. As the Commissary and the Stores officer, my job was to see that the crew ate as well as possible within the guidelines set forth. If I spent more than the allowance, neither the captain nor higher Navy brass was going to be pleased with my performance.

To retain a favorable balance between our allowance and expenditures, I seized every opportunity to augment our food supply at no cost to the 911. Such opportunities occurred in almost every harbor where we were called on to shuttle canned food from transports several miles out in the harbor to the Army and Marines on the beach. Between ship and shore, I frequently identified cases of food that I thought would enhance our menus and then had them shunted into our storerooms. The storekeeper and the cooks were also alert to our cargoes and likewise selected their choices to be taken into custody.

This practice greatly increased our holdings and trapped me in an embarrassing crisis. At the end of one quarter when these supplies were included in our inventory, the result was efficiency *par excellence*. The statistical record revealed that I had fed the entire crew of fifty-nine for ninety-one days at the staggering cost of a minus $39.10. I wanted to impress the Navy with my frugality, but this was ridiculous.

With no desire to suggest that I could perform miracles, this placed my performance in the Biblical league. I realized that Jesus had fed a multitude of 5,000 with a mere "five loaves and two fishes," but this ranged far beyond that. The statistics suggested that I had served three times as many meals (16,107) with less than nothing (a negative $39.10). Knowing that the Navy was not going to buy the argument either that I had performed a series of miracles or that my arithmetic was correct, I was left with one option; for the only time in my life, I had to falsify the record; I had to exclude from the inventory many of the cases of canned foods that were in our storeroom. Thereafter we stuck to food acquisitions through the normal channels, but we had built up a reserve that provided great flexibility in the following months.

Aside from satisfying our physical needs, food was a topic of endless debate in the wardroom. Smarba offered the most criticism although he also received the most personalized attention from the cooks and steward's mate. His complaints were abnormalities not limited to his senseless pursuit of dill pickles and his dislike of canned peaches described earlier; our handling of eggs and potatoes also struggled to make their way to the top of his list of supercilious comments, but before he exploited either, he registered an impromptu fit over the absence of napkin rings for the wardroom.

Because of his pre-war experience on another ship, he knew that napkin rings were an essential to any smooth-running operation. I couldn't understand the urgency; to that point I had never seen one; my mother never had a napkin ring in the house, but I never thought of ours as a dysfunctional family. From the captain's viewpoint, the war had to stop until he procured a set of napkin rings. He was determined that he wasn't going to sea without them. Finally for his peace of mind and the good of the war, a set was found and imprinted with an initial for each officer so that we could sally forth fully equipped to meet the enemy.

That brought a calm to wardroom life until the captain decided that his body had been bombarded with too many mashed potatoes. At noon on the fateful potato day, Smarba blurted out: "Kehl, I don't want another mashed potato on my plate for at least three days; that's a direct order." The implication was that, if I violated his wishes, I could expect some kind of punishment. Of course, the serving of mashed potatoes was governed by several factors: (a) when meat was prepared in the oven, there was no additional space for baked potatoes, but they could be boiled (for mashed potatoes) in the galley's large aluminum vat (as had been explained to the captain on numerous occasions); (b) the crew preferred mashed potatoes; and (c) every naval vessel was required to submit a weekly menu to the captain for advanced approval, and after it was signed and posted, no deviations were permitted unless endorsed by the captain.

Although a change was now dramatically authorized, I did not comment on his outburst during the meal; immediately thereafter I checked the menu adorned with the captain's signature and discovered that mashed potatoes were scheduled to be part of a meal the next day. For the reasons indicated, I decided not to deviate from the menu; I did, however, bow to the captain's personal desires but added an ironic twist.

The next morning I asked the steward's mate to scour the potato bin for the largest spuds he could find and to place two in the oven alongside the day's meat. At the same time, I was determined to tell off the captain in my own way for throwing down the gauntlet. I explained my plan to the other officers, who became willing collaborators. Mine was not a unique request; we frequently supported each other's schemes to reprimand the captain for his nonsense, and sometimes our improvisations were works of art. During my entire naval career, I was never supported more enthusiastically by my colleagues than in this instance; everyone not only participated, but also added his own expression of resentment for the captain's remonstrance the previous day.

The steward's mate excelled in carrying out his part of the scheme; he located two potatoes larger than any I have ever seen, before or since. They covered the medium-sized silver platter on which he brought them from the galley, and according to protocol, the captain was always served first. I had no idea how he would respond, but when Jackson offered him the potatoes, his eyes almost popped out. Pausing briefly, he said: "Jackson, I can't eat a whole one; please cut one in half." That was done, and the remainder was offered to the others; each of us, with a wave of the hand or a polite "No, thank you," refused the baked potato. Then when offered the mashed potatoes, each, in turn, as he was served, provided his own appraisal: "That's what I've been waiting for," "Nothing tops mashed potatoes," "This really complements the whole meal," and "My all-time favorite." In fact, we each took such generous helpings that the steward's mate had to return to the galley for more potatoes in order to serve the four of us, and our plates were so covered with the white fluffy stuff that there was little space for anything else.

No one said a word to the captain about the potato caper, but he got the message and never again returned to the topic. Nevertheless the wheels in Smarba's mind continued to turn in an endeavor to seek out new issues on which to offer

104

unbelievable perspectives, and he soon uncovered a "beaut" concerning eggs and chickens.

Even the captain could not anticipate when one of his lightening bolts was likely to light up the wardroom table. On this occasion, one of the steward's mate's thoughtful little gestures sparked the outbreak. As Jackson served Smarba breakfast, he remarked with a ring of pleasure in his voice, "Double-yolked egg, captain." Immediately the latter's chest puffed out, and he seemed genuinely honored by this special serving. Then suddenly his chin fell, his face reddened, and with his elbows resting on the arms of his chair, he began to bounce perceptively, as though he had a hot rivet in his shorts. Turning to me because, as the commissary officer, I was responsible for the food, the galley, and the cooks, he pointed out: "This ship has been in commission for five months, and this is my first double-yolked egg." Before I could figure out what was agitating him, he continued: "Kehl, your cooks have been eating all the double-yolked eggs. They might fool you, but they can't fool me."

At that moment, no one could possibly have known that his self-imposed predicament ran parallel to that faced by Captain Queeg of *The Caine Mutiny* years later. The more dramatic Queeg proposed a shakedown of the whole crew in order to find a non-existent key to the locker that contained his cherished strawberries. Smarba, on the other hand, limited his invectives to the cooks, erroneously concluding that they ate the non-existent double-yolked eggs. Although Queeg wasn't clever enough to figure out that the mess cooks devoured the succulent berries, he at least confined his search to the finite world. Smarba, on the other hand, identified culprits for an imaginary "crime."

To answer Smarba's off-the-wall assertion, I tried to assure him that the cooks were not eating better than he was and that most assuredly they were not having daily orgies on double-yolked eggs. I explained that chickens seldom lay double-yolked eggs and that, when they do, the farmer generally puts such eggs aside because their odd size would prevent them from fitting properly into the crate where, in all likelihood, they would be broken. "By some quirk," I continued, "this egg defied the odds, came to us unbroken, and ended up on your plate." But he wasn't buying that explanation.

Because my father had experimented with chickens and eggs for years, I knew a little about the subject; the captain, on the other hand, knew damned little and was gung-ho to prove it. After a brief discussion, I discovered why the captain wasn't a stellar scholar in the college of barnyard knowledge. He erroneously assumed that at least one breed of chickens regularly laid only double-yolked eggs. To him this was the only logical rationale for their existence. Almost instantly he calculated how many crates of eggs the ship had consumed over five months. Concluding that, according to the law of averages, we should have had a minimum of one crate of double-yolked eggs, he established his basis for the charge that the cooks were secretly feasting on this special hen "fruit."

Even after I shot down his misconception, he refused to surrender. "Since you seem to know so much about chickens," he demanded, "tell me how many eggs does a highly sexed chicken lay in a year?" Because sex was not germane to the thrust of his question, I let that aspect pass and answered "approximately 250." Not impressed by that production rate, he shot back: "I bet I could get them to lay more than that." By this time, the other officers had finished breakfast, excused

106

themselves from the table before they broke into laughter, and left me to end the inane discussion on my own.

Incensed by the captain's comment, I pulled out my trusty notebook and replied: "Good, tell me your secret. I'll jot down the magic formula and send it to my father who will be eternally grateful for your insight." His simple response was: "I'd put in more roosters." He thought that no egg could be forthcoming in the morning unless the rooster "humped" the hen the night before. What could be simpler? More roosters, more eggs!

I tried to anticipate where Smarba's barnyard wisdom would strike next. After pondering the possibilities for several days, I concluded that he most likely would inquire about the source of wieners or sausage. I wanted to be prepared with an explanation as wild as my creativity could conjure up, but at the same time believable to the Smarba mind.

Deciding that, no matter which he asked about, I was going to give the same answer—that links of wieners or sausage grew under a cow's left kidney, and resembling the appendix in humans, they performed no bodily function and were a throwback to ancient cows. A more challenging feat, one that I was not convinced that I could carry off, was how to keep from breaking out in laughter in the process of describing such a farce. Fortunately or unfortunately he never popped the question.

Actual "Chow Down" Menu of LSMers

BILL OF FARE FOR THE GENERAL MESS

U.S.S. _____

Week beginning __Monday, 2 October_____, 19__44__

	BREAKFAST	DINNER	SUPPER
MONDAY	Fresh fruit Fresh milk Hot cakes Syrup Dry Cereal Bread, Butter, Coffee	Baked Viennal Sausage Boiled potatoes Peas & Carrots Baked corn Cake Bread, butter, Coffee	Chili con carne Buttered string beans Steamed rice Cake Bread, butter, coffee
TUESDAY	Iced Orange Juice Fresh Fruit Fresh Milk Dry Cereal Scrambled Eggs Bacon Bread, Butter	Vegetable soup Pot roast beef Baked potatoes Spinach & eggs Buttered beets Lettuce salad Bread, butter, coffee Devil fudge cake	Italian spaghetti with meat sauce Buttered asparagus Lima beans Sliced peaches Bread, Jam, Hot tea
WEDNESDAY	Fruit Milk Oat Meal Corn Beef Hash Catsup Bread, Butter, Coffee	Pork roast Applesauce Creamed peas and carrots Mashed potatoes Succotosh Sliced pineapple Bread, butter, coffee	Beef stew Buttered beets Steamed rice Souary beans Jelly Bread, butter, coffee
THURSDAY	Stewed Figs Milk Dry Cereal Fried Pork Sausage Fried Potatoes Catsup Bread, Butter, Coffee	Spanish steaks smothered in onions Hash brown potatoes Stewed tomatoes Combination salad Pastry Bread, butter, coffee	Steamed frankfurters Boiled potatoes Boiled sauerkraut Baked carrots Chocolate pudding Bread, butter, hot tea
FRIDAY	Fruit Milk Dry Cereal French Toast Syrup, Jam Bacon Butter, Coffee	Grilled pork chops Mashed potatoes Applesauce Baked corn Creamed peas Apricots Bread, butter, coffee	Hamburger steak Hash brown potatoes Canned fruit Cream peas Buttered asparagus Bread, butter, coffee Catsup
SATURDAY	Pineapple Juice Stewed figs Milk Oat Meal Oven Baked Beans Catsup Bread, Butter, Coffee	Baked ham Boiled potatoes Boiled cabbage Boiled carrots Pastry Bread, butter, coffee	Barbecue spareribs Mashed potatoes Stewed tomatoes Buttered Beets Barthell pears Bread, butter, coffee
SUNDAY	Fruit Milk Fried Eggs Dry Cereal Bacon Bread, Butter, Coffee	Roast turkey Mashed potatoes Bread dressing Butter asparagus Creamed peas & carrots Ice cream Bread, butter, milk	Fried luncheon meat Hot potatoe salad Sliced cheese Sliced tomatoes Bread, jam, Coffee, Jello

Total estimated cost ....   Total estimated rations ....   Estimated ration cost per day ....

APPROVED: Respectfully submitted,

_____, U.S.N.,   _____ENS_____ Supply Corps, U.S.N., R
15—11580   Commanding.   Supply Officer.

108

CHAPTER 7

In American Waters

At the time I volunteered to serve in the Navy, I had never seen an ocean. On our first trip to sea from Charleston to Norfolk, around Cape Hatteras in a vicious wind and rain storm, I yearned to have my non-ocean-viewing record still in tact. During a war, one accepts the possibility of dying. To succumb to a Nazi sub or a Jap zero, although not pleasant to contemplate, was understandable, but to fall victim to the sea, as seemed certain that night off the North Carolina coast, without ever engaging the nation's enemy, struck me as ignominious. At that point, my shipmates and I did not know our true enemy, but we were abruptly introduced. The sea was to become the most unrelenting foe of our amphibious careers; only sporadically did the Japanese offer a diversion from these torments of nature.

The 911 was not rushed hastily to the front. After being commissioned in June 1944, it spent four months in shakedown, training, and travel from the Atlantic to the Pacific before

109

departing the continental U.S. for Pearl Harbor in October. Our longest layover came in Norfolk where the training was intensified.

Shortly after our arrival in the Chesapeake area with our shiny new and untested LSM, a base officer came aboard unannounced to supervise the remainder of the training that had been started before our group of men was assigned to a specific ship. He introduced himself to the assembled crew with: "I'm Lt. Mackey. I'll be with you for a week. You don't know me, but by the time I leave here, you'll all hate me." I am always intimidated when someone speaks with such assurance and, in this case, with such accuracy. His words were prophetic in every detail.

By Friday when Lt. Mackey left, we were all exhausted, frustrated, angry, and overjoyed to see him go as he had predicted; but in time, it became apparent that we were a better prepared, more confident fighting unit than we otherwise would have been. He tried to simulate crises that would confront us at sea—man overboard, fire fighting, abandon ship, manual steering, and the ever popular target practice against a red sleeve towed across the sky by a pilot who had more faith in any Navy gunner than I did. This was the only drill in which the sailors called for an encore, but all were necessary to perform and stay afloat in a war zone.

I was as pleased as anyone to see Mackey finally salute the deck on Friday afternoon and disappear down the gangway forever. One noontime, between drills in Mackey's "reign of terror," I was resting in my bunk when a boatswain came rushing in and reported to me, as officer-of-the-deck (OD) at the time, that the ship was on fire. He added: "It really isn't; some guy is timing me to see how long it takes to convey that message to you." With that he was gone again; and because there was no fire, I naively settled back for a little more rest, or so I thought.

Shortly the boatswain returned to announce that Lt. Mackey wanted to see me on deck immediately. I pulled on my shoes and reported as requested. Mackey asked if a sailor had reported that the ship was on fire. I agreed that he had, but added that he said that it really wasn't and that he was being timed. Mackey lost his patience quickly when I failed to grasp the lesson he was teaching. He asked: "Did you hear the words 'the ship's on fire' in the sailor's statement?" I confirmed that I did, but repeated the qualifier that the boatswain's mate had expressed.

Mackey wanted to hear none of that and proceeded to make the point that, when an OD hears the words "on fire," he asks no questions before sounding the fire alarm because of the importance of an early response when there is a fire at sea. After that explanation, I declared that I understood. Mackey looked at me for a moment and then blurted out: "I'm telling you the ship's on fire. What the hell are you going to do about it?" With that I sounded the alarm, and the ship went to fire quarters, the next of Mackey's drills. That's the way the week went, and it explains why the crew in general was upset at his teaching methods, but they did accomplish his goal; a group of landlubbers was whipped into a functioning crew. He helped us become survivors.

The Mackey experience was followed by a Navy decision to replace the original two 20 mm guns at the bow with a single 40 mm mount. That alteration required an additional several weeks, which was long enough for me to take several potshots of protest against practices out in the community.

The urban transportation system that linked the Naval Base with Norfolk provided the ship's personnel with an avenue to liberty. The green, squat trolleys that plied this route crossed a toll bridge that exacted two cents from every passenger, in addition to the regular fare. A special conductor boarded the trolley at the last stop before it crossed the span; then the trolley proceeded slowly as the conductor weaved his way among the passengers, mostly locals who for the most part were prepared with their pennies.

Having lived a sheltered life in Pittsburgh, a city of bridges, I had never heard of a toll being visited on passengers. After surrendering my first two cents, I groped for a means to circumvent this "panhandling" of passengers, and on my return handed the conductor a five dollar bill, vowing that I had nothing smaller. He seemed to possess neither the time nor the proper denominations of money to provide change and advised me that, for this trip, I could ride as a guest of the city.

Interpreting this as a modest triumph over the system, I decided to enlarge my experiment on the next junket via Norfolk public conveyance. Eight 911 sailors happened to be headed out to liberty on the same trolley that I boarded. This time I told the conductor that these men were all my friends and that I would pay the total assessment. I flashed a ten-dollar bill, and when each of us declared that he had no change, we all rode free. Momentarily I was the sailors' hero, not because I saved them two cents each, but because I had challenged the system, to their delight.

On a subsequent trip, I attempted to broaden the scam further. In addition to a half dozen of our sailors, there were about eighteen other Navy personnel aboard when we reached the bridge of payments. Being a big spender, I informed the

112

conductor that I was paying for all twenty-five of us and whipped out a twenty dollar bill. Can you imagine? That damned penny "moocher" was prepared for a smart-ass like me and shelled out an untidy wad of nineteen ones and a fifty-cent piece. Thus when the stakes were high enough, the system was organized to fight back.

Early in these trolley tribulations, I discovered that the transportation system was segregated. I had read about such practices but never experienced one first-hand; black people were relegated to the back half of the car, and whites were limited to the front. When a white sailor sat in the rear, the motorman told him either to move forward or to get off. Sometimes whites stood in their half while empty seats abounded in the rear, and occasionally the situation was reversed.

Because I had attended a streetcar university for four years, I knew the value of jockeying for a seat for an eight-mile ride each day; a seat in any location was a small victory won. With due respect for elderly women and small children, I had learned the art of positioning myself to get on the trolley quickly, spot, and occupy any vacant seat or identify one that I anticipated would be vacated within a few stops. To leave seats empty in one part of a trolley while passengers stood in another was foreign to my four-year ordeal; swinging from a strap with one hand and clutching a briefcase containing four textbooks with the other over an eight-mile stop-and-start ride in rush hour traffic was a condition to be avoided at all costs.

My natural instincts insisted on claiming a seat anywhere one was available. Thus I decided to sit in the rear of the trolley and thumb my nose at the system. That was more than a decade before Rosa Parks took her place in the white section of a Montgomery bus to make a statement in behalf of racial equality. I wish that I could report that I was inspired by such a lofty motive; I was simply saying that the system was nonsense to weary passengers. I'm sure that I felt more secure in my defiance than Mrs. Parks did because of my race and Navy status. Also only weeks before, I had graduated from midshipman school, where it had been stressed that, from graduation day forward, the only persons who could tell me what to do were Navy officers with more stripes than I had. Because I had only one, I was still required to answer to a lot of people, but the motorman didn't qualify.

Nothing was said about my sitting in the black half of the trolley until I was getting off; then the motorman informed me that my conduct was unacceptable. To that I pointed out that I was simply subscribing to part of my grandfather's maxim: never stand up when you can sit, and never sit down when you can lie down. I'm sure that that remark was equally unacceptable.

Of course, it was not necessary to ride the trolley. If the system was so repugnant, I could have resorted to taxis, but that mode of travel also offered pitfalls. At night in Norfolk, prostitutes often rode shotgun for many cabbies. If you hailed a cab with such a rider, you were expected to pay the fee for both. I entertained no thought of encouraging a prostitute and operated with too much Scotch blood in my veins to pay for something that I didn't use. In such a situation, if anyone beckoned a cab and the rider became visible as it pulled to the curb, protocol held that he wave the taxi on and wait until he spotted a driver who was in business only for himself. At times that made travel difficult, but such skirmishes were exhilarating and caused Norfolk to be remembered when other cities were forgotten.

When the official word came that we were leaving for Panama and destinations unknown, we were apprehensive, but from the day we all reported aboard the 911, most of us accepted the Navy's plan to acquaint us with an enemy beach somewhere sometime. For a few, that element of truth did not register until we received orders to sail with the prospect of being dispatched directly from Panama to Bora Bora without intermediate stops in other American ports. That possibility was enough to cause one of the ship's two steward's mates, Sam Shirker, to discover a pre-existing condition that could only be corrected by minor surgery, a procedure that could not be performed before our departure two days later. That was the match-up that the wily Sam wanted to achieve.

He suffered from a large wart on the side of his penis; it had been there long before he joined the Navy. It had gone undetected by doctors during two prior physicals, and it pained Sam so much that he never remembered to mention it until he was confronted with the disturbing thought that the Navy had the audacity to send him overseas. Then the pain became "unbearable," and the pharmacist's mate, who didn't believe any part of his line, advised the captain that it was nevertheless a condition for which the Navy recommended surgery.

The tall, slender, surly Sam had other attributes that were as disturbing as his appendage and his backbone. He constantly sported a blockbuster chip on his shoulder, and during our weeks in Norfolk, he had attracted the attention of the shore patrol on two occasions. I thought that his unique growth provided us with an opportunity to unload a potential troublemaker, but the captain took a much more practical view.

115

With departure two days away, he recognized that the possibility of obtaining a replacement was nil. He also reasoned that personnel centers overseas would not be well supplied with replacements and that providing a second steward's mate for a ship with only five officers would not be highly ranked on anyone's list. Thus to keep his complement full, the captain had to persuade Sam Shirker to remain on board.

In a desperate effort to prevent this transfer, Smarba's personal appeal to Shirker was novel, but not novel enough. He summoned the steward's mate to the wardroom and began with a logical argument recommending that Sam skip the operation. He argued that, within a week, the surgery would be completed and that, as inevitable as the sunrise, Sam would be assigned to another LSM with the same ultimate destination. He also pointed out, with tongue in cheek, that Sam had cultivated friends aboard the 911 and would have to make new ones when assigned to another ship.

Neither of these points impressed Sam, so the captain attempted to appeal to his vanity, advising Sam not to underestimate the advantages afforded by his fortuitous wart. "You have something that no one else has. You'll give the girls an added thrill and be popular beyond all expectations." Despite this sexual potential, Sam opted to forego the thrill and submit to the surgeon's knife.

As the captain feared, we ended up with one steward's mate for the duration of the war, a situation he had argued vigorously to avoid, but failure did not result in catastrophe; the US war effort was not impeded.

116

Tragic Twist: Sally Goes To War

On the first leg of our trek that ultimately carried us westward, we had little time to consider the steward's mate shortage. The 911 sprung a leak between its fresh water and fuel oil tanks and had to be diverted to Key West for repairs. There all hands had an opportunity to sample night club life where Sally Rand, the famous fan and bubble dancer, was the headliner.

She performed two dance routines, one clad only in two ostrich feather fans and the other in two elastic bubbles covering her strategic body parts. After two curtain calls, she agreed to autograph pictures snapped earlier in the evening at the various tables by the house photographer. With an aversion to long lines and an unwarranted smug attitude toward autograph seeking, I refused to wait to have Sally sign my photo, but a thoughtful and indulgent colleague asked her to sign both his and mine.

Behind the photo, however, lies a dramatic tale, a paradox of humor and tragedy that involved Sally more deeply in the war then she may ever have suspected. My shipmates recognized that we were not the first ship of our class to dock at Key West or the first to be entertained by Sally. One notable predecessor was the LSM 134, captained by a lawyer and would-be politician with more than a passing interest in the night clubs of Chicago, the city where Sally had perfected her fan/bubble routine.

Having entered the Navy in anticipation of combat, Captain Spike, as he was known to the crew, was originally assigned to LSM 201, designated shortly thereafter to serve as a training facility at the Little Creek Amphibious Base. In fear that he might be sidetracked and spend the war preparing others, he requested and received a transfer to a ship (LSM 134) already ordered to the Pacific. According to several members of the crew, the captain had waged an unsuccessful campaign for Congress before the war and, in anticipation of another run for the same office after the war, was anxious to compile a military record that would enhance his appeal to the voting public.

Certainly not short on courage or the love of adventure, and committed to whatever sacrifice in the name of patriotism was necessary to gain public office, he asked his political friends in Washington to pull the appropriate strings to effect his transfer to the 134. They acceded to that request, and he wholeheartedly thrust himself into the challenge. (Henry Montoye et al., *AA*, #19, 26-27.)

The gregarious captain was elated to receive a welcome from a personal friend, Sally Rand, who was now among the entertainers on hand at Key West. To return the hospitality and to provide a unique shipboard experience for his crew, the captain invited Sally and several members of her entourage to spend their off-stage hours aboard the 134. Hardly sanctioned by Navy regs, this incident quickly captured the imagination of Navy gossips, especially those aboard amphibious ships like ours; it lifted our spirits and brought excitement to our routine.

When time for the 134's departure from Key West drew near, the captain concluded that his crew should have a permanent reminder of Sally's presence among them. Arrangements were made for her artist to paint a larger-than-life picture of the dancer on the front of the ship's starboard superdecks (conning tower). Consisting of three levels, this cylinder-like island housed the radio shack, chart room, and the captain's sea cabin on the first level; the wheelhouse containing the radar, steering mechanism, annunciators, and quartermaster's table on the second; and above was the bridge with the compasses, signal light, and stations for the officer-of-the-deck and the lookouts.

The artist's totally nude masterpiece adorned much of the front of the three levels, a phenomenon that obviously created a stir among the Navy brass. When ordered removed, the mural became an instant *cause celebre*. The captain and his executive officer, to whom I am indebted for much of this detail, rose to "Sally's" defense, arguing that they were under orders to the Hawaiian Sea Frontier and would gladly replace their unique art work with camouflage paint when so ordered by that command. Nonplused by this almost arrogant response, local Navy authorities offered no rejoinder before the ship sailed with "Sally" fully exposed.

Apparently the captain and the exec, Dan Brady, were a couple of bold, fun-loving guys who wanted to test their individual wills and at the same time exasperate the Navy without being openly defiant. Described by one enlisted man as a "feisty little bastard," Captain Spike, on assuming command, stood on the tank deck on a box of canned beans and proclaimed to the assembled crew: "I'm the toughest son-of-a-bitch on this ship" and invited anyone who harbored any doubts about it to step forward and take him on. At the time, no one was aware that he had distinguished himself as a featherweight boxing champion in college, held a black belt in judo, and had served as a referee for the Illinois Boxing Commission. Wisely for all, he had no challengers—hardly the Navy approach—but he did capture everyone's undivided attention.

Smitten by the political bug with no constituency to appease, Captain Spike decided to convert his crew into one;

concern for their morale provided the driving force, sometimes merely an excuse, that veiled his reckless conduct. Impatient for combat, while the battlefront for him was still thousands of miles away and willing to substitute Navy regulations as a reasonable facsimile for the enemy, he was mentally charged for action. That combination moved Spike in and out of trouble, several times taking him to the brink, and generated non-stop excitement.

His conduct became almost legendary. On a trip back down the Potomac after a call at the Washington Navy Yard, where Admiral Ernest J. King and General George Marshall inspected LSM 201 as an example of the Navy's newest assault weapon, the captain docked at Quantico and invited a group of lady Marines aboard for a dance. Later he delighted the crew in an even more tangible way when he ignored Navy orders and granted leaves to everyone. As an appropriate encore, he thrilled most of those aboard when in one sweeping action, he bumped every enlisted man up one rate (except those already holding a first class rating) without regard for examinations or time in grade.

Dan Brady, on the other hand, possessed a totally different temperament; also a daring risk-taker, he preferred to overcome any adversaries in his path with a facile mind and lucid argument. Together this pair declared themselves winners in the tiff with the Key West authorities and confidently anticipated round two in the next port.

That opportunity came with their arrival at Colon in the Canal Zone. Confronted with a similar demand to remove Sally's likeness, the exec became the spokesman for their celebrated painting. Having recently been enrolled in a law school program at the University of Virginia, anxious to hone his skills, and buoyed by the Florida experience, he vehemently argued that the 134 was subject only to directives from the Hawaiian Sea Frontier. Although this argument lacked merit, he sustained it long enough for the ship to receive orders to proceed to San Diego, an assignment that in the midst of war took priority over "Sally's" impending demise.

Once in California, "Sally" became an immediate target of port officials. A tough-minded, no-nonsense submarine captain, with sea salt in his nostrils and barnacles on his ass, was temporarily assigned to inspect all LSMs as they passed through on their way to the Pacific front. When presented with the Hawaiian Sea Frontier litany, he exploded. Announcing that he would return the next day to complete the inspection, he warned: "If I see 'Sally' tomorrow, a formal reprimand will be issued." His expectation that "Sally" be painted into oblivion was agonizingly clear and almost stymied the intrigue.

With a little lunacy in their hearts, the captain and exec, as committed stewards of the art entrusted to their keeping, found refuge in the words "if I see Sally." Desperately attempting to twist the inspector's order and thereby salvage "Sally," they reasoned that, because the submariner's only dictum was not to see her, why not hide her from view?

At this point, accounts of "Sally's" survival differ. One maintained that Captain Spike decided to cover "Sally" with paper and paint the paper with the intention of removing it once the final inspection had been conducted. That stratagem failed when the paper tore, and a second attempt substituted light canvas for the paper. Unfortunately according to this version, the naval authorities learned of the captain's defiance and ordered him courtmartialed. Appealing to the commandant whom he had known in Washington, Spike escaped punishment,

121

but his ship was ordered to proceed immediately to Pearl Harbor. (Montoye et al., *AA*, #19, p. 27.)

Another interpretation held that "Sally" was covered with grease, not paper or canvas. The purpose was to create the illusion of a glossy paint job that was so expertly applied that it deceived the inspector who cleared the ship to sail. Once out to sea, the crew rolled out the fire hoses and washed "Sally" down. With a thin film of grease still adhering to her body, her more distinctive points shone brighter than ever in the sunlight.

Our ship followed the same course as the 134, making the same ports-of-call. Always hearing about the 134's splendiferous conning tower but never rendezvousing, we never gazed on this specimen of feminine pulchritude and stoically accepted our fate. The saga of "Sally," the nude who rode above the waves, was, I am sure, magnified with each telling as the story circulated throughout the amphibious fleet. Unfortunately I am unable to separate fact from fiction because the spectacle of "Sally" always remained a phantom, never sailing within range of my searching binoculars.

The 134 went on to participate in the landing at Leyte Gulf and tragically suffered numerous casualties. A 75 mm shell scored a direct hit on "Sally's" left bust and ripped a hole into the bridge. Years later the pharmacist's mate who attended to the wounded and dying that afternoon recalled for me the nightmarish obstacles that he had to overcome to minister to those in need. Every piece of equipment on the bridge was mangled, confusion reigned among the crew, and "the blood ran deep"; he knew because he "kept slipping in it." The casualty list ultimately reported three sailors dead and severe shrapnel injuries to four others, including the captain whose Navy career was abruptly ended. After receiving treatment for fifty shrapnel wounds to the right arm and both legs, he returned home to Chicago. The arm was paralyzed, and one foot partially so, but when reminded that he would never referee a fight again, he exclaimed: "What the hell . . . I'm back." (*Chicago Tribune*, January 13, 1945)

Until D-Day on Orange Beach at Leyte, the "Sally" incident was regarded by Spike and his crew as one great spoof of Navy regulations. For his role in the crisis, the exec was awarded the Silver Star, recognition for his heroic deeds in supervising the care of the wounded and retracting the ship from the beach under enemy fire. Years later when Dan Brady and I discussed the invasion, he exhibited pride in the Navy ribbon hanging on his living room wall but confided that, for him personally, the "Sally" painting was a prank that had gone too far. "Sally" may have been good for morale, but ultimately she may have contributed to the disaster.

His reluctance to talk freely about the incident implied a sadness over the fact that "Sally's" glistening breast presented a more definable target than anything else along the beach that afternoon of October 21, 1944. If "Sally" had been obliterated in San Diego or at any other point before the ship reached the war zone, perhaps the 134 would have escaped without casualties, a thought that has haunted Dan ever since.

By the time we had put into Key West, the scene of "Sally's" origin, our officers were preoccupied with a more serious concern; they had tentatively concluded that the 911 would be better off without the captain than with him, but we had no idea how to accomplish that feat. Allotted fourteen days availability to have the ruptured tank repaired, the captain took off to visit his wife in Miami.

123

When the job was completed in ten days, I thought I could exercise a little leverage to leave the captain behind because the assistant port director had been one of my university Latin professors. I suggested to him that he order us to sea because the repairs were completed. He maintained that, since the 911 had been granted fourteen days for repairs, he could not send us forth before that deadline expired.

He did offer a glimmer of hope by pointing out that, after the two weeks had elapsed, if the harbor were congested, he might be persuaded to act. Unfortunately on the thirteenth day Smarba returned, but during that Key West layover, it seemed to me that the crew was getting better adjusted to each other and to life aboard a floating cork; nonetheless the saga of captain versus crew continued. After we set sail again and passed the Panama checkpoint, the 911 was routed to California, not Bora Bora, where additional training at both San Diego and Long Beach occurred before we said adieu to civilization as we knew it and set our compass for Hawaii.

CHAPTER 8

Combat Fallout

Over a violent and critical eighty-two-day period in early 1945, the United States launched its final three devastating assaults against Japanese-held islands. The first was in Lingayen Gulf (January 9) and the third at Okinawa (April 1); the LSM 911 participated in both, but missed the daring Marine invasion of Iwo Jima sandwiched between the other two.

Even before the 911 reached Pearl Harbor on its circuitous route to the Philippines, I became dramatically aware that we were rapidly catching up with the war. Although the action was still several thousand miles away, it sounded loud and clear on the ship's radio. On October 25 an excited petty officer called me into the radio shack to listen to a distress call from an American ship. The simple, agitated message, without any pretense of resorting to code, underscored how urgently help was needed. The plea for assistance from any unit in the area revealed the troubled ship's latitude and longitude, and the

125

frantic voice described how his vessel and others in the convoy were being fired upon from the rear by a Japanese battle fleet; the shells were falling short, but the pursuers were closing the gap rapidly.

That report caused my heart to skip a few beats. Without knowing its significance at the moment, I was hearing an on-the-scene description of the first phase of the crucial conflict in the Philippine Sea, the greatest battle in modern naval warfare. An enemy fleet had emerged from the San Bernadino Straits, off the island of Samar, to surprise unprotected escort carriers and oilers, thereby triggering "the most gallant naval action in our history, and the most bloody." (Morison and Commager, *The Growth of the American Republic*, II, 832.)

By the time we sailed from Pearl Harbor, we knew the outcome of the battle, but it was a most sobering experience. We did not head toward the eye of that naval storm, but toward the South Pacific where it had already passed. Our first destination was Funafuti (Ellis Islands), long a British possession, and at the low point in the war the lone Allied outpost between Hawaii and Australia. Locating that island required precise navigational skills; with only a few palm trees standing more than a few feet above the water at high tide, it was not readily detectable, but strategically it provided a closed anchorage and a reprovisioning depot rimmed by coral reefs. From there we were routed via Tulagi to Bougainville where we boarded the Army troops and equipment that were ultimately delivered to the beaches at Lingayen as a part of the master plan to push the war closer to the Japanese homeland.

In the captain's absence I supervised the loading of five tanks, two jeeps bearing piper cubs (with wings detached), and one bulldozer; basically these pieces of equipment were lined up

126

in a single column on the main deck with the bulldozer at the bow and thus the first to be disembarked. Before the captain returned to express his displeasure, all were lashed down with chains and turnbuckles in anticipation of rough seas.

As a kid, Smarba had a casual acquaintance with a bulldozer that chronically sputtered and stalled. He generalized from that one youthful experience: bulldozers as a class are temperamental and their engines might conk out without warning. By my arrangement of the vehicles on the deck, no equipment could be moved from the ship until the bulldozer exited; that frightened him.

Exclaiming that he did not intend to become a sitting target on any enemy beach while Army personnel tried to coax a "cranky" bulldozer to "get up and go," he demanded that all the vehicles be unloaded and reloaded so that the suspect piece of equipment would be the last to leave the ship. In that position it could not hinder the departure of the tanks and jeeps. The change turned out to be one of the captain's better decisions during the war.

When the 911 ultimately reached the Lingayen shores, the tanks and jeeps rumbled speedily off the bow ramp; under full throttle the bulldozer also charged the beach, cleared the ramp, and immediately sank in four feet of water and stalled out. As he predicted, the captain raised the ramp, retracted from the beach, and "got the hell out of there." Thus the reloading, based on limited evidence, paid surprising dividends.

The day after boarding the Army in Bougainville, we departed for the east coast of New Guinea where, with other ships of the strike force, we rehearsed not only the invasion procedures, but also alternatives that might be utilized if the originally-selected areas were not swept clean of submerged mines. Once that exercise was completed, we moved to Manus in the Admiralties where we spent Christmas and took on our final provisions before heading north to the Philippines.

An Unconventional Christmas

For most of us aboard the 911, this was our first Christmas away from home, a holiday experience that is generally one of the more memorable in an individual's life. Although neither unique nor traumatic, it nevertheless bordered on the dramatic. Between 1941 and 1945 large numbers of individuals faced their first separation from family and friends at Christmastime. When our turn came in 1944, many others were already enduring their second, third, or fourth consecutive holiday observance away from their families because of the war.

Arriving in the Admiralties on December 22, we could not blot from our minds the January 9 date in Lingayen Gulf in spite of the fact that the Navy tried to create a relaxed atmosphere. This was to be the first invasion for all aboard the 911, and although anticipation hung like a cloud over the Christmas celebration, the occasion was outwardly festive. Despite being at a remote outpost, the cooks served a traditional turkey dinner topped off with a five-gallon can of mixed nuts. Half the ship's company was granted liberty in the afternoon, and the availability of free liquor at the Officers Club seemed inviting to the officers.

When Captain Smarba declared his intention to take advantage of the club's open bar, he automatically confined the other four officers to the ship. Although only the officer-of-the-deck was required to remain aboard, we had a pact never to be seen socially with the captain, and the Officers Club was the only attraction ashore. He may have liked it that way as much as we did because over the first few months that the ship was in commission, he never invited any of us to join him for a social evening. Events that unfolded thereafter prompted our resolve to retain the status quo.

To say that relations between the captain and the four officers were strained was no understatement. Although everyone acted professionally in public, the undercurrent was obvious, and Christmas did not alter sentiments. To the spirit of goodwill to all men, the officers and crew alike, unfortunately, made one exception. At the outset the captain had enjoyed the respect of all hands, but discordant notes over the months engendered an antipathy that could not be easily erased or set aside.

The captain was not oblivious to prevailing attitudes, but I'm not sure that he had any interest in redressing them. If he did, he pushed all the wrong buttons, and his actions further alienated everyone because his conduct squeezed every ounce of humanity out of the respect that was once his.

In part, the captain's insecurity can be attributed to his lack of rapport with people. All four of the officers had performed manual labor during their college days and had at least a modicum of finesse in relating to members of the crew who were called upon to carry out the physical work aboard ship. The captain, on the other hand, experienced only a brief stint in the workforce as the driver of a dry cleaner's truck. When he caused the truck to become too intimate with a tree as it rounded a curve, he was fired during his first week on the job.

None of the officers was willing to accompany this Dale Carnegie dropout to the Officers Club, but elected to remain on board; we exchanged thoughts on holiday traditions in our several families and wrote a few letters. All was serene until the men began reporting back from liberty at an hour that coincided with the closing of the Officers Club.

Although the free liquor had pumped the captain's blood alcohol content to the point that he was glowingly mellow, he nevertheless decided to stop at the Fleet Post Office en route back and pick up the ship's official correspondence, known as Guard Mail. Staggering toward the dock to catch a boat out to the 911's anchorage, he relaxed his grip on the numerous letters and packets that the post office had provided; escaping his notice, individual items began to fall from his hand. Fortunately some of the crew were following the same route to the dock and recognized the inebriated captain littering the roadway with mail. They tried to retrieve what they could and turned their collection over to the officer-of-the-deck when they reached the ship.

Delivery of the mail was far less challenging than maneuvering the captain from the boat to the ship which could be boarded only by a Jacob's ladder, a steel contraption with chain sides and pipe rungs that hung down from the deck to the waterline. Use of the ladder required dexterity in two feet and two hands; failing in all four necessities, the captain was doomed to be hoisted aboard in a cargo net. He smiled and nodded approval as several sailors pulled the rope on the davit that bounced him up the side of the ship and onto the superdeck.

Once that mission was accomplished and the captain assisted to the wardroom, we shut the door to seal the spectacle from the crew. At first undecided about how to handle the situation, we left the captain leaning against the closed door. Before the officers reached any conclusion, he slid down the door until he was sitting on the deck. We stood him up again, but gradually he slipped back down.

My personal feelings were mixed. On the one hand, I was angry because I realized that no punishment was going to be meted out, but if someone else had arrived in such a novel conveyance, he would have been confined to quarters for the foreseeable future. On the other hand, I was amused because I had never before seen the captain bombed out of his gourd. As I wavered between the two attitudes, Smarba, feeling no pain and conscious enough to detect a quizzical look on my face, slurred: "There stands Ensign Kehl as sober as a judge," and slid back down.

Aware that the captain was oblivious to the conversation taking place around him, the officers tried to outdo each other in posing clever questions for him. One asked: "Who spiked your turkey?" Another admonished the captain: "Didn't you check the alcohol content of your turkey before eating it?" But the most ingenious wanted to know: "Did you get the cork out of your turkey, captain?" Alert enough to know that this was the worst attempt at a metaphor that he had ever heard, Smarba smiled and began his slow descent to the deck once more.

After the cleverness had run its course, the exec recommended that we put the captain to bed. I countered with the thought that we let him sit on the deck to contemplate his navel when he gained consciousness. The exec prevailed and stuffed him, fully clothed, into his bunk.

In the morning we waited for a reaction—to discern what the captain could recall about the previous evening and what questions he would ask. Remaining in his cabin to read the recovered mail that had been placed on his desk, he kept us in suspense until almost noon. Disheveled, red-eyed, and nervous, he emerged with a battery of questions pertaining to his conduct as a mailman. That was far more important to him than his arrival via cargo net because the mail contained numerous confidential communiqués concerning the Lingayen Gulf invasion. During the evening's ordeal we had paid no attention to the mail and had not, therefore, speculated on its importance.

Landing sites, naval units involved, assault tactics, and the invasion date were all revealed in these confidential memos. One significant piece of the puzzle was missing: the hour at which the assault was to begin. Although the duties of each unit were spelled out, all actions were described in terms of a specific time, designated only as H-hour, which was to be set forth in a separate memo. Certain maneuvers were scheduled to occur at H-minus three hours, and others at H-minus one hour, with the invasion itself taking place at H-hour followed by supplemental actions coming at H-plus one hour, etc. Nowhere in the recovered mail was there a memo defining H-hour.

Its absence raised the captain's anxiety quotient and prompted him to inquire in detail about his return from the post office. He remembered that he had picked up the Guard Mail, but how it reached his desk was a mystery. Still unaware of its importance, we embellished the sailors' accounts of chasing down wayward envelopes. Spurred by that revelation, the captain confided that the memo setting forth H-hour was missing. Thus, our comments reinforced his suspicions that the memo was an item not retrieved.

Because his inebriated condition, replete with cargo net, was the talk of the ship, it could not be covered up in the event the Navy conducted a general inquiry into the memo's disappearance. The captain admitted that such an investigation was possible because the loss compromised Navy security and placed the total invasion force at risk. A blunder of such magnitude was a courtmartial offense, and Smarba already pictured himself exchanging his Navy blues for the horizontal stripes of either the Leavenworth or Atlanta federal prisons. Since the captain had shown no compassion toward us at any time, we were not thoroughly distraught over such prospects, but no one ventured to ask if he preferred incarceration at one over the other.

By mid-afternoon the captain had regained his composure, recognized that the absence of the document had to be reported to the OTC, and sent a message stating the loss. He revealed simply that the memo was not included in the 911's packet of materials and skillfully lobbed the ball into the OTC's court with the hope that he would let it drop. The reply was prompt and terse: "Said item omitted from all packets. Will be supplied only after all units are underway."

With that revelation the captain was off the self-created hook and remained aboard for another five months. One of the sailors later confided that the crew had expected the cargo net experience to "humanize the bastard." That didn't happen; the crew versus the captain relationship did not change, but recollections of that Christmas in the Admiralties has remained vivid for many of us after fifty years. Every time I see or hear the World War II slogan: "A loose lip may sink a ship," I am inclined to add a second line: "But a loose grip on the mail might a whole fleet imperil."

The Combat Zone At Last

D-Day at Lingayen was almost uneventful for the 911, but we didn't know that would be our fate until nightfall. We arrived that morning well in advance of H-Hour, and the captain proposed to anchor five or six miles out in the Gulf. His order to drop the stern anchor was complied with, but the ship continued to drift. Since my battle station was at the stern, he asked over the phone system, that included all crucial points of the ship on one circuit, what was wrong. Thinking that I could relieve a little of the tension we all felt, I replied: "Captain, I think you dropped it in a hole." Some laughed, but not the captain. Then I reminded him that the water was probably a mile deep and that the anchor cable wasn't half that long. Thus it dangled behind the ship.

During the first night in the Gulf, the Japanese equivalent of our frogmen swam out, attached small charges of explosives to the propellers of several ships, detonated them, and left the ships helpless in the water. Before darkness set in the second night, the Navy took steps to defend against a repeat performance; all ships were advised to double the watch at night and to shoot anything that floated, be it can, box, or human.

During that second day we were kept busy ferrying men and supplies from the large transports to the shore. Just before dusk we took on a load of high octane gasoline in fifty-five-gallon drums (approx. 20,000 gallons). Then 100-125 soldiers came aboard and were invited to find comfortable seats on the drums for the short trip to the beach. Immediately after we pulled away from the transport, all ships in the harbor were alerted for an air raid. The Army personnel expected us to make a mad dash for the shore, but Navy procedure maintained that, when under attack or anticipating one, ships should continue underway or anchor several miles off shore until the crisis passed. To the discomfiture of the Army, we dropped the anchor. None of us was overjoyed at the prospect of facing an

134

air attack with this highly volatile cargo—especially the soldiers who needed no reminder that they were seated on something with the potential to provide a much bigger bang than the defective exhaust system on Uncle Louie's '37 Buick.

Part of the Navy defense against an air attack called for laying down a smoke screen that would hopefully envelop the whole harbor so that the outline of individual ships would not be visible from the air. The order came "to make smoke;" for us that was a signal to start our smoke generator designed to convert oil into smoke at a rapid rate. This piece of equipment was located at the stern, and ours was as undependable as the captain considered all bulldozers. With no provocation this proved to be one of its more temperamental times; oil was coming out the nozzle without being completely atomized. As a result it sprayed a thin film of oil on the deck, stanchions, and cables in the immediate area.

Assuming that the generator was about to stall out and that we could rely on smoke from other ships to cover us, I recommended to the captain that we shut it down before its parts were permanently damaged. I realized that continued operation was dangerous, but not how dangerous. Thinking that he was giving priority to the protection of our inflammable cargo, the captain angrily refused my request: "When I want smoke, I want smoke. I don't want excuses; I want smoke."

That response was positive enough for me to keep the generator running without further comment, but eventually a spark ignited the coating of oil on all the stern's metal surfaces and burst into a ball of fire. The darkness of night caused it to look more menacing than it really was. Within a minute the blaze was extinguished, primarily because the film of oil was quickly burned off; in addition, as a safety precaution several crew members were standing by with a fire hose in the event of such an emergency and immediately sprayed the area and all of us who were in the midst of the blaze.

Those few seconds that the fire raged were long enough for eighteen of our Army passengers to decide that they no longer appreciated our hospitality and jumped over the side. The instant the fireball lit up the sky, the captain shouted almost hysterically through his megaphone from the bridge: "Put foam on it, Mr. Kehl. Put water on it. Do something." This advice wasn't much help; foam would have been a mistake, and our crew already had a spray of water going.

From his battle station at the bow, the exec witnessed the same impending danger. He immediately set out to make his way over the drums of gasoline toward the stern to assist in combating the fire. His progress was impeded by panicked soldiers groping aimlessly about in the darkness atop the drums. As a result of his inability to move rapidly among these terrified troops, the blaze was extinguished before he got there.

In the meantime, unable to communicate with the captain by phone, I was making my way from the stern to the bridge to report to him on what had happened. The exec saw me coming over the barrels, and before I recognized him, he grabbed me around the waist, lifted me off my feet, swung me around, and exclaimed: "Congratulations! How did you get it out? What went wrong?" We almost lost our balance at that moment and fell in a heap; only the press of the milling soldiers kept us on our feet.

Of course, I had done almost nothing and couldn't appreciate his impassioned concern since I knew the true nature of the fire which was destined to burn itself out quickly. The impression from both the bridge and the bow was that the ship had sustained an explosion of undetermined origin at the stern, and from the exec's perspective we had achieved the impossible in bringing it under control. When the pyrotechnics fizzled, the Army swimmers were anxious to re-think their hasty leap for safety and again sought refuge aboard our not-too-cozy, but eminently dry, deck facilities. Although our crew members heaved a few life preservers in their general direction and launched a life raft, their return was much more complicated than logging in after liberty.

Miraculously, in spite of the darkness and the man-made fog, all eighteen made contact with a life ring or the raft, but a swift current was carrying the raft away from the ship. At first the Army boys could not locate the paddles in the raft and then discovered that they lacked the skill and cooperative effort to direct the raft toward the ship. More importantly all ships in the Gulf had been ordered to shoot anything in the water, especially individuals, because of the Japanese demolition antics the night before.

The captain wasted no time in alerting the fleet to the fact that the soldiers had forsaken our companionship for a nighttime swim. Without delaying to codify the message, he went on the radio and in plain language announced: "The LSM 911 has survivors in the water." That word "survivors" had an unfortunate connotation.

As was frequently their custom, the Japanese had dispatched a plane to monitor the attack: to assess its success and to make certain that the pilots didn't drop their bombs and/or torpedoes in the sea and return home without engaging the Americans. That plane intercepted the captain's message and assumed that the 911 had been damaged, if not sunk. When the observer plane reported our supposed demise to Tokyo, that message was picked up by Navy monitors on the West Coast, and a few of our families thought that the 911 was in the company of Davy Jones.

Meanwhile, the captain's prompt action gave the soldiers a reprieve and prevented them from becoming a target to Navy small arms fire, but they had failed to master the problem of the current which was still carrying them farther and farther away. We put a rowboat in the water, and two sailors volunteered to go to the Army's rescue. They quickly got close enough to throw a line to the raft and began the Herculean task of towing it back to the ship. We cut down the distance by paying out anchor cable in order to move the 911 closer to the "survivors," but in attempting to assist in the recovery effort, the soldiers often complicated the problem. Trying to pull the raft with most of the eighteen inside it or holding onto its sides, the sailors made grudging headway against the current. By the time they reached the ship, they had major blisters on both their hands from gripping the oars and on their backsides from slipping on the seat as they worked to gain the leverage necessary to pull the oars through the water.

Almost fifty years after that leap and rescue, an infantryman from an Anti-tank company wrote a letter in the LSM newsletter, *Alligator Alley* (October 1994), asking if anyone could corroborate his "first experience with shear panic." He was one of the soldiers seated on our cargo of gasoline when the flash fire broke out and described how "men jumped and dove into the water." Four of us from the 911 recognized his description and individually wrote to answer his question: "Where are the men in this story today? I want to shake the hand of the skipper and the . . . sailors of the unknown Landing Ship Medium."

This infantryman described how, immediately on recognizing the crisis, he took a position at the starboard rail; with his feet hanging over the side and an arm hooked around a stanchion, he planned to jump "when the first drum of gas pops"—a truly bad plan. If he waited that long and if the fire had reached the gasoline, the explosion would have propelled him into space. Fortunately that pop never came, but he lost circulation in the arm while clutching the stanchion and "slipped into the sea" where he and the others floundered for two hours.

By the time the rescue was completed with all hands accounted for, the air raid had ended, and we retired for the remainder of the night with the soldiers once again resting uneasily on the gasoline drums. The impromptu swimmers were accorded special privileges: were ushered to the crew's quarters, served hot coffee, treated to a shower and dry clothing, and as one infantryman chronicler later remarked: "It was great to be alive." We provided breakfast in the morning before landing them on the beach, but they were obviously more appreciative of the sand and mud under their feet than by the flapjacks under their belts.

Sleeping for a few hours after the highly charged events of the night before, the captain wasn't sure that he wanted to permit the two Army officers who had joined the jumping party to walk away without a reprimand. He maintained that they should not have jumped without an order from him to do so. Our Navy officers argued that all who went over the side had been motivated by self-preservation and their conduct should be excused, but such comments did not assuage his anger.

His assumption was that, if they hadn't jumped, the enlisted men would not have done so; thus there would have been no incident in which we were forced to compromise part of our security at a time when we had a hazardous cargo. He warned us: "If one of you had done that without my order, I'd see to it that you were courtmartialed. Nothing less should happen to them," but ultimately realizing that he could exercise no direct control over Army personnel, he settled for simply being nasty to them during their final hours aboard.

In the course of our ten-day stay in Lingayen, the Japanese alternately annoyed and amused us. During the days we laughed at the ramblings of Tokyo Rose and after dark we were harassed by Japanese planes that roared high overhead with nothing more menacing in mind than forcing us out of our bunks and onto our battle stations as often as three times a night.

Tokyo Rose addressed her daily radio visits to the Army and Marines who were on the shore. Picking up her signal, we overheard her prophesy of doom for all American forces because they had been dumped off and deserted by the Navy. According to T. Rose's scenario, ships that had not been sunk were scurrying back to the safe harbor at Guam.

While listening to this diatribe, we on the 911 were quietly executing our assignments between the transports and the shore in the midst of the invasion fleet that was still present—operating at will with only meager daylight challenges from the air and no Japanese ship was within a hundred miles. Hers was a fabrication that frightened no one and brought a smile of satisfaction to many.

On the other hand, the Japanese offensive at night struck a discordant blow to our morale; it showed no respect for our preference to enjoy eight hours of uninterrupted sleep. Flying at high altitudes, generally with no plans to drop any bombs, these planes served no other purpose than to force all ships to awaken their crews and send them to general quarters for as long as the Japanese intruders remained in the area. After thirty to forty-five minutes, the planes would fly off, only to return about the time they thought most sailors were again snug in their bunks.

This attempt to psych us out did achieve limited success; some did become weary and others cranky, but for the most part everyone took this diversion in stride. Some sailors thought that they could actually distinguish between the engine sounds of the two most regular harassers; not knowing the official classification of these planes that they never saw and only heard, our crew nicknamed them Washing Machine Charlie and Piss-Call Paul, often cursing them by name as they headed toward their battle stations where they continued their friendly arguments about which of the two was actually tormenting us at a particular time. That lessened the tedium as we waited in place for action or for an all-clear.

The Enemy's Last Stand

By the time the ten days were up, we welcomed the order to withdraw to Leyte only to discover that the fly-by fad played a role in the nightly routine there as well. We likewise learned that the tempo of the war was shifting into overdrive. Within weeks another invasion was slated for an island with the strange-sounding name of Iwo Jima. We needed a map to locate it and were genuinely surprised to find that such a speck did exist on the earth's surface, but soon learned how significant that speck really was.

Excused from that invasion, the 911 was informed that the master schedule called for us to participate in still another, planned for an island with the equally unfamiliar name of Okinawa. Situated in the Ryukyu chain, it also represented a gaping hole in our geographical knowledge. When we realized that it was north of Formosa, long a rock in the Japanese defense that was being bypassed, we knew that this was serious stuff.

After ferrying supplies around the Leyte area (Tacloban, Ormac, Dulag, and Cebu City) for almost eight weeks, we loaded a medical unit and headed for Okinawa—arriving on D-Day, Easter Sunday, April 1, 1945. As at Lingayen, we played no spectacular part in the initial assault, but our later operations in the area did add several footnotes to the American success.

Because of the change in Japanese strategy that involved a decision not to contest the beachheads with the invading force, the Marines captured more territory the first two days than they expected to acquire in a week. As a result ammunition that we put ashore at the landing site was needed twelve to fifteen miles up the coast; the most efficient way of hauling it there was to re-load it aboard the 911 and transport it by sea.

Night began to fall as the Marines re-stocked our main deck with their artillery shells. Unfortunately this activity coincided with a Japanese air attack, something the Navy hoped to avoid with ships on the beach. Too late to comply with the preferred guidelines, the 911 remained in place to fulfill its assigned mission.

I had never witnessed a night bombing before. As I stood on the fantail, I could not imagine what was making those streaks of light in the sky. Tracer bullets went up, but these were less distinct and were descending. I had little time to ponder their significance before the first of a series of bombs hit the water. I hit the deck, but the concussion caused the stern to

142

rise up to meet me on the way down. Before I shook off that jolt, succeeding bombs landed in the water, and with each the stern alternately rose and fell. Through the whole process I was out of sync, going down when the ship was going up. When the complete series of "eggs" had been laid, I picked myself up from the deck and found a piece of shrapnel lodged in my life jacket— my closest call during the war.

Our nightmare did not end with these near-misses. Although this was the closest the enemy attack ever came to the 911, that night also marked our only battle casualties. In the course of other ships' firing at the Japanese bombers, a stray small-caliber bullet probably from an American gun landed in our port guntub amidships. After whirling around the inside of the tub, the bullet struck three sailors, sending two to the hospital. That caused everyone's heart to skip a few beats or as one sailor expressed it later: "We all pissed ourselves over that one."

When we had hit the beach to take on the Marine ammunition, the ship came to rest half on a reef and half hanging over its edge. As the tide ebbed and the loading of shells weighted it down, the 911 cracked in the middle to the extent that certain deck plates split open. Since this happened at night, after all the other excitement had subsided, I was in my bunk; the deck of the wardroom sprung open and fuel oil from the tank below bubbled onto the deck and covered it with six inches of oil. My first awareness that something was wrong flashed across my mind when I saw my moccasins float out the door.

Only half awake, I first thought that the ship was sinking. I slogged my way through the oil, up the ladder, and onto the main deck where the loading was methodically progressing. Once alert to this revolting development in the wardroom, the captain concluded that the shells already loaded represented our capacity, waited for the tide, delivered the ammo to the Marines up the coast, and scheduled the 911 for maintenance that was quickly forthcoming.

Ordered to undergo repairs at Kerama Retto, a small but strategic group of islands only twenty miles west of the port of Naha near the southern tip of Okinawa, the 911 remained there for two months. The Navy had shelled that area a few days before the Okinawan assault, destroyed the installations, and swept the harbor clean of suicide boats. This action effectively cut off the enemy survivors who took to the hills, primarily on Takoshiki-shima, the largest island that formed one side of the archipelago. Zamomi-shima was the only island in the group completely secured, and part was promptly converted into a military cemetery. No attempt was made to occupy the other islands; the Navy's interest extended only to the protected waters which, in turn, provided a forward repair base, a reprovisioning depot, and a home for reconnaissance sea planes and their tender.

After our repairs were completed, we were assigned as part of the reprovisioning detail with a specific responsibility for dispensing fog oil. A large cargo vessel dropped all of its fifty-five-gallon drums of oil on our deck, and as ships of the fleet needed to replenish their supplies, they were instructed to dispatch their small boats to our anchorage for a pick-up. We serviced their needs from our lowered bow ramp by simply rolling the requisite number of barrels onto their boats.

This was a necessary but mindless task. For excitement the sailors suggested that they train at least one 20mm gun on the Japanese soldiers whom they could observe lurking on the mountainside. Because there was no imminent danger, the idea

144

was rejected, especially since an American ship, anchored between the 911 and the shoreline, would not have viewed this as a friendly act.

When that ship moved, sailors revived their request and were given permission to fire at moving targets. The captain's decision on the subject can be defended from several angles: we wanted the enemy to understand that we were aware of his presence; and there was always the possibility that the Navy had failed to capture or destroy every single suicide boat—no need to give the impression that we would not be ready if one headed our direction.

On several occasions our boys fired a few bursts into the hillside, but the Japanese took great care to expose themselves a little as possible. The prospects of having an opportunity to fire kept the on-duty crew alert, relieved some of the boredom inherent in our role as oil dispenser, and perhaps helped keep the enemy from trying to exceed his capabilities.

The most ominous threat came not from the islands, but from the sky. That realization was dramatically demonstrated on the evening of April 28 when a major catastrophe struck. As a sea plane was returning to Kerama Retto from a scouting mission, it failed to detect a Japanese Val bomber flying on its tail. The Val was so close that ground radar picked up only one pip. By the time the reconnaissance plane dropped down for its landing, it had unwittingly escorted the enemy bomber over the harbor undetected.

Selecting the largest ship in the fleet as its target, the Val took a suicide dive into the USS *Pinkney* (PH-2), a hospital evacuation ship. (According to the Geneva Convention the United States was allotted a fixed number of hospital ships permitted to be painted white with large red crosses on either side and thus immune from enemy attack.) The need for hospital facilities was greater than American authorization for protected ones; thus the *Pinkney* was functioning as a ship of mercy, fully armed because it faced all the wartime hazards of fighting ships.

The Val's bomb penetrated four decks to the engine room and immediately disabled the water and electrical systems. This rendered the vessel helpless to fight the fires that broke out on the various decks as a result of the explosion. At the same time that the crew called for assistance from other ships to extinguish the fires, the failure of the electrical system generated heroics on the part of two doctors. They had just made an incision on a patient to perform a routine appendectomy, or so they thought, when the lights went out.

Realizing that they were trapped below deck, temporarily at least, the doctors proceeded with the surgery. One held a battle lantern (high-powered flashlight) while the other performed the cutting and suturing. Burning oil in the next compartment caused the interfacing bulkhead to glow red from the heat and its paint began to curl. By the time the doctors had successfully completed the surgery, a firefighting party reached the scene, led them to safety, and transferred the patient to another ship.

The 911 was one of several ships ordered alongside to fight the fires aboard the severely-crippled *Pinkney*. Not trained for this kind of duty, Captain Smarba and the rest of us relied on instinct and common sense. Pulling along the port side of the stricken vessel, the captain ordered the crew at the bow to get a line over to the *Pinkney*. My talker at the stern reported what was happening, and since the ships were now parallel, I presumed that the captain intended for us to tie up at the stern as well, certainly the most favorable position from which to transport fire hoses and personnel to contain the fire. With sailors on the *Pinkney* desperate for aid, I also concluded that in the excitement the captain had forgotten to give the order for us to get a mooring line across. That proved to be a false assumption on my part, but when no order came, I acted on my own and had the sterns lashed together.

Shortly thereafter the ammunition in the ready boxes on the deck of the *Pinkney* began to explode, caused either by the heat or the actual fires; bullets were sprayed in every direction. Sailors on the stricken ship scattered to take cover, and not knowing how long and with what consequences this ammunition was going to burn, Captain Smarba decided to pull away. Only after he ordered the bow line to be cast off did I inform him that we were also tied in at the stern with no one available on the *Pinkney* to disengage us. At that point Smarba was not happy with me; without resorting to the phone system, he yelled: "Get an ax! Get an ax! Cut that line!" Before I could comply, the ammo from the ready boxes was spent, and the immediate danger subsided. The 911 remained tied to the *Pinkney*; our fire hoses were quickly in service, and our crew began fighting their way into the ship.

The combination of water being pumped in and damage from the suicide dive caused the ship to list to starboard, but in the darkness this was not evident until the angle was so severe that the vessel was in danger of capsizing. We tried to pump water over the side in order to correct the list, but our equipment was not powerful enough. After approximately two and a half hours, with all fires extinguished, our boarding party was recalled, and we returned to our anchorage and left other, better equipped ships in charge of stabilizing the *Pinkney* for the night.

We later learned that this evacuation ship was caring for 100 patients at the time of the attack, and nineteen of them were numbered among the thirty-six fatalities.   Fifteen died in sickbay. I recall opening the door to one ward where nothing seemed disturbed; a deathly stillness prevailed; all were victims of smoke asphyxiation in their beds.

For a few of the casualties the attack represented double jeopardy. They had recently come to the *Pinkney* from the cruiser *Wilkes-Barre* where they had been the survivors of an explosion inside a gun turret. As reported by a crew member from a ship that evacuated personnel from the *Pinkney*, these men were already "bandaged from head to toe from burns. We even lit their cigarettes for them and put them in their mouths and took them out because they were unable to do it for themselves."   After enduring this second life-threatening experience within a few days, they were ultimately transferred to another hospital ship. (Joseph Fields to James A. Kehl, September 16, 1992.)

The 911 boarded no survivors. In spite of the heroic deeds of crew members who fought the fire, we also experienced an embarrassment. On this most crucial of occasions that we faced during the war, the services of our pharmacist mate were urgently needed, but not available. A seasoned veteran of the North Africa campaign where he contracted malaria, he suffered chronic attacks of fever and excessive sweating which he attempted to alleviate with an unauthorized, self-prescribed elixir composed primarily of torpedo juice. On this fateful evening he was bombed senseless and unable to assist anyone, including himself.

Omitting this incident in his report to the Task Force commander, Admiral I.N. Kiland, Smarba took pride in mentioning that "not a man flinched and all hands conducted themselves in accordance with the tradition and high standards of the Naval Service." In response, with a copy to Admiral Turner, Kiland declared: "The prompt assistance rendered by LSMs 911 and 96 in fighting and extinguishing severe fires aboard the *Pinkney* on 28 April saved many lives, as well as possible destruction of the ship. Your courageous and efficient actions are greatly appreciated. Well done."

This *Pinkney* incident was the most challenging of our stay in Kerama Retto/Okinawan waters. After an exhausting three months we received orders to return to the Philippines to transport several Army units to Okinawa. This assignment was promptly carried out, and we were back in Okinawa when the atomic age was ushered into our consciousness at Hiroshima and Nagasaki.

When the capitulation of Japan was rumored, we found ourselves in the midst of the wildest of worldwide celebrations marking the end of the most encompassing war in history. On that night of August 11 the sky was bright with a display of light that surpassed any July Fourth demonstration. Search lights, signal flares, and tracer bullets randomly criss-crossed the heavens in a menacing exhibition intended as jubilation. Tensions were released, inhibitions forgotten, and exuberance ran unchecked; anyone with ready access to a gun began firing indiscriminately. In the morning after the merrymaking at Okinawa subsided, the tragic toll rolled in: 100 casualties, including six fatalities.

When this fireworks in behalf of peace began, orders on the 911 were for all ammunition, Very pistols, and other firearms to be locked up to prevent members of the crew from joining in the riotous outbursts. I personally watched the display briefly and then headed for the safety of the wardroom. Although the end to hostilities had not yet been verified, my attitude was that, if I had lived through the conflict to the armistice we all desired, I was not going to take a chance on getting killed celebrating it.

When general quarters sounded the next evening, the thought that the celebration was a little premature raced through our ship. In spite of the expectation that the war had ended, all ships in the harbor were sent to their battle stations. The 911 was given an additional order: to make smoke to cover the USS *Pennsylvania*. Our temperamental generator responded flawlessly, but the winds refused to cooperate. We circled the battleship several times and even threw smokepots into the water, but the elements defied our best efforts, ones that had worked before. When the task proved impossible, the 911 was ordered back to its anchorage inside the smoke-covered area— leaving only the *Pennsylvania* clearly visible to enemy aircraft if indeed an enemy still existed.

A Japanese pilot who had not heard or would not accept the peace rumor took advantage of the battleship's exposed position and launched a torpedo into its starboard side causing more fatalities than the Mighty Penn had sustained at Pearl Harbor. Tragic as it was, this bombing marked the final gasp of a vanquished enemy; at last the guns grew silent, and everyone began to think more positively about returning home.

Combat Fallout

Winding Down

Peace did not readily translate into civilian life for most of us. Occupation of the Japanese Empire required many ships, included the LSM 911, to transport men and supplies to various ports throughout China, Japan, and Korea, but after two runs into Yokahoma the long trek home was underway. We were dispatched to Guam which pointed us in the desired direction, but there I experienced my first major disagreement with Naval authorities. When the Navy would not relent, I left the 911 and turned myself into the base hospital for elective surgery that had been postponed for eleven months.

Although made in anger, that proved to be one of the better personal decisions during my Navy career. About the time I was to be released from the hospital, I looked for a temporary duty station because only the Bureau of Personnel in Washington could re-assign me permanently, a process that could take a week to three months.

Fortunately I discovered that the Naval Operating Base (NOB) administered a unit called Educational Services (ES) that provided correspondence courses to military personnel throughout the Pacific Ocean Area. Since that activity sounded closer to my chosen career of teaching than any other office on the island, I inquired about a temporary assignment there—in an office run by middle-aged college professors who had received direct commissions based on their professional standing and buttressed by a minimum of orientation about Navy procedures.

About that time, the ES office found itself facing a potentially embarrassing situation unless a person like myself could bail them out. Coxswains operating small boats in Guam's Apra Harbor had become undisciplined, and accidents were commonplace. On the average one boat was sunk every day to the consternation of the island commander. In a dictum setting forth his displeasure, he declared that after January 1, 1946, no boat would be operated in the harbor without the coxswain having a special island license. Such permits could be obtained only after an individual passed a course in boat-handling. ES was requested to design and teach such a course, and once this policy was in effect severe penalties would be assessed to anyone guilty of violating the rules of the road.

Not even knowing that there was a protocol to be followed in ship/boat crossing situations, the ES administrators were about to convey their ignorance of this fundamental when I appeared at their doorstep. They immediately recruited me to fulfill the command that they had been given, but I needed no recruiting. This was my first opportunity to see the inside of a classroom since I had been commissioned, and I latched onto it with gusto.

ES and I embraced each other. I was given space, personnel, and the full cooperation of everyone. All the various bases on the island clamored to enroll their coxswains because the more qualified operators they possessed the greater their flexibility in carrying out assignments. No one took lightly the word of the commander; only licensed coxswains were tolerated henceforth.

Success with this program caused other offices to turn to Educational Services for help. Because a high percentage of storekeepers and yeomen had accumulated seniority over enlisted men in other classes, they were among the first to accrue enough points for discharge. Directives stipulated that they be rotated to the States to be mustered out even though no replacements were sent to fill the void. Offices on Guam suffering from this dearth requested through the Personnel Office that ES set up a facility on location to train individuals in these specialties. As with the training of coxswains, the ES administrators lacked the requisite skills in these fields and asked me to add this responsibility, which I readily accepted.

In order to make certain that I would be permanently assigned to ES, the director wrote a strong letter to the Bureau of Personnel, routed through channels, stating how essential it was to have continuity in the functions that I was fulfilling. Thoroughly happy with this statement, I was at last doing what I thought I could do best and looked forward to remaining in that capacity until eligible for discharge when I could fly home without any mickey-mouse jobs en route.

Since the request was not returned to Educational Services, the proper presumption was that it had been forwarded to Washington. Protocol held that Captain Ivan Odor, the NOB commander, must return it to the director if he disapproved. ES and I were pleased when several weeks elapsed and the request had not been denied, but a month later I received an engraved invitation to report for re-assignment to sea.

Although not as disturbed as I was, the ES director asked the NOB commander for an explanation; in my mind he was fast becoming the SOB from NOB. After babbling for a few minutes, he opened the center drawer of his desk from which he unveiled the original request that he had deliberately sidetracked and never sent. Complying with neither of his legitimate options (forward approved or return), he unsympathetically commented: "It would have been turned down anyway" and considered the issue closed.

The director quietly accepted that answer, but I requested a personal interview. When I tried to use established Navy procedures as my argument, Odor immediately became defensive. The rule that I invoked maintained that an individual's commanding officer (Ivan Odor, in this case) may request a verification of a Bureau of Personnel order. His admitted mishandling of the original request, plus the success of my school programs in the interim, prompted me to press vigorously for a reaffirmation from Washington. His response was characteristic of his attitude: "Did you ever hear of a man by the name of Nimitz? He tried that from here and was turned down. What makes you think that you have more pull than he did?" My rebuttal, I thought, was thoroughly logical. "Although Admiral Nimitz may have been turned down, I have no knowledge of the circumstances. Since you never rejected nor forwarded the original document, I think that I do deserve that courtesy." He dismissed my argument with a simple "No," and I exploded.

His parting shot that day was "If you open your mouth again, I'll have you courtmartialed." I figured I was outgunned at the moment and left. Never after that was my attitude toward the Navy quite the same. I had been given an opportunity to work in my field and I acquitted myself well; in fact, when I departed, Educational Services presented me with a letter of commendation.

After leaving Odor's office, I looked out over the harbor and noticed LSM 145, swaying at anchor. In my midshipman school days, I had had a friend who was later assigned to the 145, and I wondered if he was still aboard and if by chance his ship needed an officer in this period of rapid change caused by postwar downsizing.

154

After the horrible morning with Captain Odor, it turned into my lucky day. I went aboard, discovered that my friend who was now the captain, needed both an engineering and an executive officer, and was leaving for the States in several days. Although I knew nothing about the mechanical operation of an LSM, I volunteered to fill both slots. A deal was worked out with the Personnel Office, and I was assigned to the 145.

On the afternoon before we were to head eastward, when officially no longer under Ivan Odor's command, I went back to convey to him my unadulterated sentiments now that I considered the "playing field" relatively level. I simply proposed to sound off and walk out. I reasoned that, before he could react officially, the 145 would be underway.

Fortunately for both of us perhaps, he wasn't in his office, but when his assistant asked if he could be of service, I rescued a little pleasure from my disappointment by asking him to extend a heartfelt farewell to "that pompous horse's ass with four stripes." I walked out as planned, and temporarily felt relieved for having unloaded on him, but despite my many positive feelings for the Navy, I cannot erase the negatives of the tiff with Odor from my memory. During the next four months of delightful duty aboard the 145, my actions were at times defiant reactions to the Guam affair; I made a covenant with myself never to permit Navy orders to take precedence over my personal preferences if there was any way to prevent it.

LSMers home and duty station.

Boatswain Archie LaFrenierre captures the spirit of the captain's
seamanship.

CHAPTER 9

Return from Pearl

Novelist Thomas Wolfe wrote that we "can't go home again." Although correct in his philosophical context, these words were overwhelmingly rejected by the millions who served overseas during World War II. Actually the antithesis of Wolfe's dictum became the cornerstone of American morale. During wartime tedium, everyone boasted or daydreamed about a particular place and a specific way of life to which he yearned to return. Everyone assumed that "God willing, I can go home again." Without that "carrot," the war would have been pointless from the perspective of the individual serviceman. Certainly the attitude on my homeward trek was typical and did not conform to Wolfe's conclusion.

On a February morning in 1946, the thoughts and dreams of the preceding year and a half were coming clearly into focus. From the bridge of our amphibious ship, as we approached from the west, I could see the outline of Diamond Head looming more distinctly with each passing minute. Although not the lady with the torch or the strands of a Golden Gate, this imposing mountain on the distant horizon was perceived as a huge billboard flashing a cordial "welcome home."

With trepidation I had departed from the safe confines of Pearl Harbor months before and was now returning years older aboard the LSM 145 as its executive officer/navigator/engineering officer. We were not scheduled to pass Hawaii's most picturesque landmark for several days; our orders called for a logistic stop at the Pearl Harbor Naval Base which lay to the left as we closed the distance to Diamond Head. Our ETA from Guam was noon on Lincoln's birthday, but because we were several hours ahead of schedule, I ordered the engine room to cut the speed to one-third. After traveling for fourteen days at the agonizingly slow rate of twelve knots, the speed reduction created the illusion of a ship dead in the water. Slowing the approach to Pearl allowed me to savor the moment—to reflect on the past and to daydream more positively about the future than I had dared to do before.

Until this trip from Guam, I had never navigated a distance of 3,300 miles without sighting land. A great inner satisfaction came more from doing it than from the complexity of the challenge. Anyone who had passed Navigation 001 could have reached the destination on schedule. The ocean had been calm, and every morning and evening the heavens had provided excellent opportunities for star sights, but I found a personal pleasure in reflecting on the actual accomplishment.

Until I saw the outline of Hawaii's majestic mountain, my thoughts were only idle dreams. In those final hours, as we seemed to glide toward the harbor, my mind focused on what I would do once the Navy career ended; I had already concluded that my primary goal was to return home, attend graduate school that summer of 1946, and begin a master's program in history. My desire to teach had been sidetracked by the war but not diminished; more than ever I was eager to teach at any level. I assumed that I would teach in high school but dreamed about a college-level appointment. I also realized that, being bound to the 145 for the duration of its days in the active fleet, I might not be discharged in time to meet my projected schedule without some luck or conniving. The months ahead proved that both were needed.

In the midst of daydreaming that morning, I remembered to notify the captain that land had been sighted. In response he requested that I "flash" the tower when appropriate and ascertain the uniform of the day at the Navy Base; (protocol held that the crews of visiting ships were expected to wear the same uniforms as base personnel).

In my happy, almost giddy frame of mind, I assumed that he was jesting—proof that I had been away from the civilized Navy world for too long. Without calling the tower, I sent back a scribbled note saying: "Jock straps and shoulder boards for officers, no shoulder boards for enlisted personnel." Within thirty minutes he wandered up to the bridge and in his laid-back, southern drawl politely informed me that his request was not intended to be frivolous. To this day I do not understand his point; he was not a by-the-book officer, but I got the message, both his and the one from the tower.

In the months since I had gone to the forward zone, the uniform of the day had been any reasonable facsimile of officers' garb that I wanted to wear; everyone else, especially those on small ships, adopted a similar dress code. The captain had been back in the more formal realm of the Navy since I had; that may have refreshed his memory on the proper etiquette while mine had continued to rust.

His insistence on knowing the proper uniform shocked me into realizing that Pearl Harbor was different from other ports into which I had sailed over the previous sixteen months; this was no Funafuti, Bougainville, Tulagi, Tacloben, Cebu City, Dulag, Manus, Okinawa, or Kerama Retto, places where I had been assigned in the interim. I had no disdain for Pearl Harbor; on the contrary it was special to me, but not as a facility that observed Navy protocol; it was the *cause celebre* for waging the war, and we were now returning, satisfied that "the date which will live in infamy" had been avenged.

We entered the harbor properly clad and were ordered to moor temporarily off Hospital Point, alongside the destroyer escort, *Ulvert M. Moore*, commanded by Franklin Roosevelt, Jr. That suggested a point for Thomas Wolfe: most of us had been from seven to eleven years old when Commander Roosevelt's father first assumed the presidency; we had grown up and gone to war knowing no other president; now conditions had changed; we were returning home at ages twenty to twenty-four with another resident in the White House. Before I could meet the ship's captain whose name was familiar to every American household, we were assigned a permanent berth in which to anchor and moved farther into the harbor, past the sunken hull of the USS *Arizona* where more than 1,100 of its crew members were entombed forever, a perpetual reminder of what happened there on December 7, 1941.

Once I heard that we were being relegated to West Loch, all daydreaming was indefinitely suspended. The mere mention of that remote part of the harbor jerked my mind back to reality. In October 1944, aboard LSM 911, I first became painfully aware that assignment to West Loch spelled exile. For a small ship with no boat of its own to ferry in supplies and crew members to liberty, this was a social Siberia. Relying on a base-operated shuttle service of small boats, movement from ship to shore was an ordeal not to be forgotten. Standing on the hot, steel deck of an LCM for an hour with no railing to hold onto, provided the only requisite elements for an agonizing adventure. Although I didn't think that being sentenced to West Loch was discrimination, I felt that we were being punished for being the Navy's newest creation.

As I reflect on that berthing assignment, I realize that the Navy was not discriminating against the amphibious fleet. Being the most recent addition to the Navy's strike force, landing ships had to take their place at the end of the line which in this instance meant an anchorage farthest from the operating base. On land the command center experienced a similar fate; the headquarters of Admiral Turner, who shaped the amphibious strategy for much of the Asiatic-Pacific theater, was also an outpost—at the end of a long row of buildings that housed longer established administrative functions. But, I was in no mood to accept rational explanations and resented the impediment that West Loch presented.

On the few occasions when I had to go to the main part of the base during our brief stop in Pearl Harbor, I grumbled about the inadequacy of the "land package," as well as the water travel. By the final trip I was more than slightly annoyed and registered my displeasure by exhibiting a cavalier attitude toward base regulations.

Ashore, "leaping lenas" provided the basic mode of travel except for the private cars of "top brass." Comprising a fleet of tractor-drawn flat-beds that never stopped, and moving slightly faster than one could walk, these conveyances plied established routes. As one passed by, passengers jumped on and off at the desired offices or intersections where they could conduct business or board leaping lenas headed in other directions. A fellow passenger, uncertain of his facts, advised me where he thought I should leap off to catch another flatbed for our headquarters that functioned under the lengthy title of The Administrative Command, Amphibious Forces, Pacific Fleet and known simply as AdComPhibsPac. The intersection where I leaped off was in the middle of nowhere, and I had no idea when a leaping lena headed in my desired direction would come along or if indeed one traveled that route.

My first impulse was to hitch-hike, a no-no for naval officers, but frustrated by the whole situation, I didn't care. I waved my thumb frantically for a few minutes before my eyes detected an approaching car, empty except for the man behind the wheel; distinctly displaying three stars on the front license plate, it denoted the vehicle of a vice admiral. Assuming that the admiral's driver would never stop for me, I immediately withdrew my thumb from circulation. He sped past but slammed on the brake. I ran up, climbed into the back seat, and suddenly realized that I had jumped into a potential lion's den.

I found myself being chauffeured, not by an obliging sailor, but by the admiral himself. In a gruff, admonishing tone conveying that he was aware that I had violated the hitch-hiking rule, he asked: "Where are you headed?"

"To the Administrative Command, sir," was the reply in my most respectful Navy voice. Turning his head toward me to reveal the three stars on his collar, in case I had missed them on the bumper, he shot back: "I *am* the Administrative Command."

162

My chauffeur was Admiral Lawrence F. Reifsnider, who had recently relieved Admiral Turner. Electing to make no "big deal" out of my errant thumb, Reifsnider proved to be a delightful, thoughtful man who attempted to put me at ease by asking questions about LSMs. Professing to know little about amphibious ships because this was a new type of assignment for him, he obviously regarded this as an opportunity to learn first-hand. He interrogated, and with fear and apprehension, I provided the answers. (During my Pacific stint I had never encountered an admiral in the flesh—no one above the rank of captain.)

The admiral asked what was bringing me to his command. I told him that I needed a release and routing orders from his port director for the LSM 145 to proceed to the States. As the car approached his headquarters, he explained that he would point out the appropriate office. Realizing that the improbable spectacle of a junior officer being squired by an admiral was about to be unmasked before all those gathered at the front of the Administration building, I became more uncomfortable than ever. When the car stopped, his aides rushed to open doors for both of us. They saluted the admiral, and when he returned the salute, I did likewise. To my knowledge no one laughed or even smiled at this oddity.

Calling on a part of my midshipman training that I had never used, I followed one step to the rear and a few feet to the left as we entered the building and went up the stairs. The admiral flung open the door to a room in which approximately twenty personnel were at work. Immediately someone called "Attention!" and everyone stood up; commanding them to "carry on," the admiral pointed to a lieutenant commander in a

163

far corner and said to me: "That's your man"—loud enough for all to hear.

In an incoherent stammer, I thanked him and headed to the corner as directed. The officer waiting there had no idea whether he was being approached by the admiral's nephew or a home town neighbor, and I decided to keep it that way. He asked in a polite, particularly solicitous tone: "What can I do for you?"—a novel question for a port director. In my experience such individuals were often more dictator than director due to the demands of their positions. His question implied to me that my entrance with Admiral Reifsnider had intimidated him, and for the first time in any port director's office, I felt in triumphant control of my destiny.

When presented with the dispatch ordering the LSM 145 back to the States, the port director asked: "Where do you want to go?" To me that was further proof that I was in charge; port directors *tell* not only where but also when. Without hesitation I answered "Long Beach" because I knew that harbor better than San Diego's. His second question, instead of an order, was "When do you want to leave?"

"Wednesday morning at 0800" was immediately on my lips. Without equivocation the orders were cut to my specifications; eager to deliver the good news, I found the leaping lenas and boat trip back to the 145 in West Loch absolutely exhilarating.

With our departure set for Wednesday AM, the initial phase of my summer school plan was falling into place more easily than anticipated. Once I reached the ship, my attention focused on a newly emerging obstacle. After arriving at Pearl, our radiomen informed me that, while monitoring their designated channels at night, they overheard illicit radio transmissions among LSM radiomen about ships already in California.

Apparently all LSMs judged seaworthy upon arrival in West Coast ports were being quickly reprovisioned and sent on an extended voyage through the Panama Canal to rendezvous with their decommissioning fates at Charleston or Norfolk. My 1944 trip from Norfolk to Long Beach had taken a month, and to retrace that route would consume a similar period of time. Suddenly my schedule for graduate study was in jeopardy if this added travel were required; it became imperative that I find a way to short-circuit the Navy's intention.

Our radiomen reported sad tales of ships that had served overseas for long periods being shunted off to Atlantic ports even though manned by a high percentage of sailors who had accumulated enough points for discharge. I cautioned against participation in such conversations because their unofficial nature could result, if participants were identified, in severe punishment, a complication that could slow decommissioning and discharges for all of us.

That admonition was based on my recall of a dramatic occurrence at Kerama Retto seven months before. With few official radio transmissions at night, several radiomen sought to relieve the boredom with some unofficial ones of their own. I remember hearing a radioman puncture the silence by asking: "Anyone here from Chicago?" After a pause a second voice admitted: "I'm from Chicago."

With that the two exchanged pleasantries about the Windy City—exploring various topics in an effort to discover common ground. The discussion ranged from high school football to teenage hangouts and from the opening of the upcoming baseball season to the city's all-time sports heroes.

Then with several germane comments the City's third representative introduced himself as "Chicago 3," and a network began to take form.

Eventually Communications Central interrupted this gossipy session with a stern warning that this breach of security could result in a protracted visit to a federal penitentiary. For the moment that halted all discussion, but after a few minutes a reflective voice declared "at least I'd get m' mail there."

When the same kind of personal dialogue resumed the next night, Communications Central was prepared. With direction finders mounted on several small craft, officers circled the harbor, zeroed in on specific ships, walked aboard unannounced, and caught radiomen engaged in their back-fence chitchat. I had no idea what punishment was meted out, but I knew that I did not want our sailors to be arrested in a similar escapade.

I nevertheless suggested to the radiomen what information could prove valuable: What materiel condition would warrant decommissioning at the port of entry? Did port authorities consider the length of a ship's tour of duty overseas in making a determination? Was the number of miles logged on the ship's engines a factor? These were among the numerous questions I posed, and, swearing they never inquired, only listened, the radiomen generally supplied cogent answers by the next morning.

As need dictated, the Navy published ALNAVs, communiqués to all ships and stations. In addition to the radioroom scuttlebutt, the key to our plan for a California decommissioning was to be found in one of these publications. It directed commanding officers to conduct detailed inspections of their ships' materiel condition and report the findings to

166

Admiral Ernest J. King, Chief of Naval Operations (CNO), along with a recommendation indicating whether the ship should remain in commission. The captain and I debated the meaning of that particular ALNAV. Did it include amphibious ships such as our LSM or only major ships of the fleet?

We concluded that it did not apply to us, but I suspected that we might be able to twist its contents to our advantage by assuming that LSMs were included and addressing the requested assessment to CNO. The captain endorsed my scheme to report an ironclad case for decommissioning on the West Coast. We did not want the Navy to conclude that, since the 145 had completed the second leg of the 5,500-mile trip from Guam to Long Beach without a breakdown or major incident, another 4,700 miles to Norfolk would exert no particular strain.

Knowing that there could be no reaction from CNO before decision-time at Long Beach, I had to find a way to prevent assignment to Norfolk from being transformed into an official order. Thus a memorandum to Admiral King was merely spinning our wheels, but a cleverly worded copy of such a statement, when waved before Navy authorities in Long Beach, would imply that the original was on its way and might intimidate them. My ploy was not to send the original to CNO immediately, but to mail it later only if the Navy was obtuse enough to deny our request for a California decommissioning.

Information supplied by the captain, plus the ship's records, provided the sources for a two-page memorandum that I put together. Careful to describe only conditions below the waterline that could not be checked without drydocking, I assembled a report of structural weaknesses that graphically described a ship that might sink while standing at anchor. M y

167

history of the ship's deteriorating condition began with its duty on the beaches of Iwo Jima where "cargo operations, a four-foot shell hole, and a hurricane necessitated the return of this vessel to the United States for a two months' availability" [repair period].

The original repair plans called for the "removal and replacement of all plating, frames, and longitudinals on the port side of the ship to within eight or ten feet of the keel." Because of the urgency to return the 145 to the Pacific to participate in Operation Olympic, the projected invasion of the Japanese homeland on November 1, 1945, "The port side was removed and replaced only down to the waterline," a quote from the ship's records that I exploited in the CNO memo.

The report further stated: "The stem of the ship is broken, and all strength members, baffles, and plating from the stem back to frame five are beginning to accordion. The stiffeners bracing a bulkhead between two forward ballast tanks have sheared off because of this faulty bow." Additional detail underscored the fact that: "Since leaving the United States in September 1945, we have had six breakdowns at sea," one caused a fire and another, a steering failure, "almost resulting in a collision." I concluded the argument with a simple statistic: "Since July 1945 the vessel has spent more than fifty per cent of its time undergoing repairs."

None of the items noted in the memorandum was a complete fabrication; all were documented or suspected by me or the captain. Perhaps I overstated the ship's state of disrepair beyond the factual evidence, but after I saw the sheared parts of a six-inch beam in a forward void (a tank purposely kept empty) move four or five inches as the 145 plowed through calm seas, fear spawned an exaggeration that required little creativity.

As I re-read that memo today, it seems very professional although I've forgotten the distinction between baffles and stiffeners. The suggestive power of my words was so strong that I began believing the memo and was a little hesitant to cast off all lines lest the ship sink before we cleared the harbor. But, when the sun came up on Wednesday morning, such thoughts were shoved into the background, and we departed on time, determined not to waste my lucky encounter with Admiral Reifsnider that permitted an early get-away.

Saluting Diamond Head, we set our course for Long Beach and enjoyed an uneventful voyage until the last day at sea. The overcast sky on the day prior to our scheduled arrival provided no opportunity for a sun line at noon or star sights at night from which to develop a fix on our position. The next morning was even more disappointing from a navigational standpoint; enveloped by fog, the California coastline offered a forbidding, inhospitable welcome. We were obviously in the general vicinity of Long Beach, but no landmarks were visible. Expecting the fog to burn off by noon, we were wrong again.

Although the war in the Pacific had been over for eight months, this turned into one of my most terrifying days in the Navy. Once more my mind whirled, not in anticipation of civilian plans, but with thoughts aimed at preventing a potential catastrophe. Perhaps I was overreacting, but collisions at sea usually occur near congested harbor entrances, a condition made more hazardous by the fog surrounding us. Visibility was less than thirty feet beyond the bow of the 145, and a lookout was stationed there throughout the day. We sounded the ship's horn frequently to warn away any vessel in the immediate area.

Return from Pearl

Groping at minimum speed in fear of what lay beyond that thirty-foot limit, I understood some of the anxiety that Columbus's crew must have experienced on its first voyage; they feared falling off the edge of the earth, but to me the unseen danger was an accident and its repercussions. With all the land clutter, our radar was not sophisticated enough to detect the harbor mouth; my navigational instincts must have been reasonably accurate though, because the 145 was observed on the radar screen at the base which radioed in late-afternoon: "Are you having difficulty?" What a relief—just to know that someone knew where we were, especially since we didn't. With our affirmative response, the base replied: "Stay in that position; a pilot will be dispatched." It seemed only minutes before his small boat arrived alongside; he took us directly to a dock where our cargo of landing crafts was unloaded.

Before that task was completed, the scenario reported by the radiomen at Pearl Harbor began to unfold. An officer who outranked both the captain and me came aboard to offer assistance in getting the 145 underway for a trip through the Canal and an ultimate berth in the mothball fleet. Except for a brief stroll on the dock, I hadn't yet enjoyed the luxury of being "home," and this expediter was already plotting my exile for another month or so.

Partly because of the expediter's pressure and partly by design, the captain and I haltingly rambled about the 145's seaworthiness before I casually injected: "We have a comprehensive study of the ship's condition that was prepared for CNO. I'll get you the ship's copy." We could not anticipate the reaction to our list of proposed repairs necessary to make the ship seaworthy but knew that no one could logically dispute the "reported" damages without drydocking, a needless expense since the ship was destined for decommissioning somewhere. Sufficiently confused, the expediter departed to consult his superiors but promised to return the following day with a definite answer to our fate.

With our memo to Admiral King purportedly "on the record," the base decided not to challenge our assertions of damages sustained by the 145, and the ship received permission to be decommissioned there. We never knew if those responsible for seeing the light accepted the accuracy of our report, feared a reprimand if we were ordered out in an unsafe condition, or concluded that it was not good economics to risk a breakdown at sea. In any event we were instructed to leave the unloading dock and stand by for our turn to tie up at the decommissioning pier.

Clouds with Silver Linings

With no specific anchorage assigned, we selected the berth most advantageous for us and simply moved the ship to the end of the dock where we had unloaded—which happened to be a condemned area owned by the Hammond Lumber Company. The location was ideal; it afforded direct access to the highway and to transportation into the city of Long Beach. That, in turn, placed the wonderful world of Los Angeles within striking distance of every sailor via the Pacific Electric, an interurban train that whisked the crew to and fro with almost every liberty. If we had anchored in the harbor, we would have been forced to repeat the old familiar pattern of dependence on an irregular harbor boat service to reach shore for both business and pleasure; the Pearl Harbor experience was still fresh in our minds, and no one wanted a repetition of that.

In an attempt to secure our position at the condemned pier indefinitely, I visited the port director's office at once to report our location and in the process learned that the chief petty officer in charge was married and lived off the base, that is, in the civilian sector where luxuries such as steak and butter were still in short supply. I invited him to come and inspect how safe our location was for our purposes; the heaviest object we intended to take across the dock was an oversized sailor with an overload of beer in his belly. The chief came, saw, and was rewarded with a package of steaks, a pound of butter, and an invitation to re-inspect as often as he felt duty demanded. The meaning was clear; only the dense could fail to grasp my intent, and the chief wasn't dense.

The captain and crew were relatively content, having imposed no deadline on themselves such as a date with summer school. Good liberty was readily accessible; the Navy made no specific demands on our time, considering us in a holding pattern until ordered to move to the decommissioning dock.

No one took greater liberty with liberty than Frank Lee, our third officer. Although the LSM complement generally included five officers, after the war we were reduced to three counting Lee who didn't count for much. Having first been assigned to sea duty after V-J Day, he recognized that his service-time was destined to be short. As a result he wanted to pack as much frolicking as possible into that brief period and considered liberty a fulltime occupation.

A twenty-one-year old from downstate Illinois, Lee had not yet been fully weaned from childhood. He acted as though every day was a new burst of freedom from parental control. At breakfast he repeatedly bragged to the captain and me about the beautiful women he had drunk with the night before.

172

We didn't want to hear his tales; as a result we debunked all his comments—suggesting that he could not attract any girl over sixteen except a brain-dead Amazon. Good naturedly we would say: "To see is to believe; bring one around sometime and we'll give you a professional opinion; until then let's not hear it." Neither of us thought he would attempt to comply.

Lee's iron-railed bunk was alongside mine, only a foot away, with tiered bunks above both. One morning, half awake, I opened one eye and caught a glimpse of something dangling over the side of the bunk above Frank's. Since no one normally slept there, I thought to myself: "What the hell is that?" A quick second look confirmed that it was a human leg, not male. Lee had brought his pickup from the night before back to the ship for our inspection and to demonstrate that he was indeed adept in attracting women. I pretended to be asleep so that I could take full advantage of any explanation offered later.

Lee and the woman quickly left the wardroom and then the ship. I dressed and nonchalantly walked up the ladder and over to the gangway where the sailor on duty stood. I initiated the conversation by asking if he saw anything strange that morning. He was elated to have such an opening.

Smiling broadly, the seaman admitted that he had observed an odd one and asked: "Did you see the woman Mr. Lee brought aboard last night?" I shook my head in the negative because truthfully I hadn't seen much of her. He then explained that she was more than twice his age—"at least fifty and downright ug-glee."

The captain and I concluded that Frank had a beer problem: after two he was still able to distinguish between men and women, but beyond that his vision was uncommonly fuzzy. By morning's light and with a clear head, Frank realized his mistake; the woman he met the night before was transformed from a pleasant blur to a distinct someone whom he was embarrassed to introduce to the two of us, thus the reason for shuffling her off the ship before we were up and around.

The incident was the final proof in convincing me that Frank Lee was bad news. Since his lack of knowledge about the ship's equipment meant that he would be of little assistance during decommissioning, I argued that he should be transferred ASAP—before we had to answer to base authorities for his ill-advised conduct. The captain agreed, and in two days he was reassigned to become someone else's irrepressible headache.

Regularly checking our position on the decommissioning list, I concluded that we were advancing too slowly and needed a plan to expedite an early end to our Navy careers. With the 145 tied up at a dock instead of riding at anchor out in the harbor like most other ships, we were in a unique location to take charge of our own destiny.

The theory behind the decommissioning process was that all gear would be removed systematically from each ship and stored in a specific locker on the base. If an emergency necessitated recommissioning the vessel, all the essentials would be readily available in one place. Acting on that theory, I convinced the authorities to assign a locker to the 145 before our appearance at the decommissioning dock so that we could begin typing the required invoices to remove and store smaller items. Thus the crew members not on liberty on a particular day could assemble and truck spare parts, sick bay supplies, fire-fighting gear, navigational charts, guns, and other equipment to the locker. Permission was granted, and I was happy knowing that every item transferred would shorten the time required for formal decommissioning.

One afternoon, after several days of steadily shipping equipment to our storage area ashore, the ship received an unexpected and disheartening order by radio to proceed to the Eleventh Naval District headquarters in San Diego for decommissioning. At the time we had no hint that such action was contemplated, but apparently my insistence on speeding up the decommissioning process caused a glitch in communication between the Long Beach base and the district headquarters. The latter was unaware that we had transferred any equipment ashore, and we on the 145 never realized that my attempt to circumvent Navy procedure contributed to the confusion.

Dismayed and almost speechless, I concluded that a horrible error had occurred; half-walking and half-running, I hurried to the Long Beach base to have my assumption verified. Instead, I was advised that the information was correct and that we should prepare to depart. Hearing that was a tonic to my speech. Arguing animatedly that, with part of our gear already ashore at Long Beach, it would not be accessible if recommissioning in San Diego were ever called for. My logic failed to impress. With callous indifference the authorities responded: "We don't know why; we don't care; we only know that you're one less ship with which we have to contend."

That was enough to stimulate my blood, and I asked to see the chief who had eaten my steak (I was beginning to take this personally). Informed that he was unavoidably elsewhere, I didn't believe that statement for a minute and lost my cool. Aside from the incident on Guam, I had kept my temper in check out of respect and pride in the Navy despite the fact that regulations were frequently frustrating and exasperating. Although never defiant during the war, I developed a much shorter fuse after V-J Day. Now infuriated by the order to

175

move south and by the lack of empathy for my cause, I made it eminently clear that I had no intention of going anywhere to find myself at the end of another long decommissioning line without a helluva fight and stormed out.

Back at the ship the captain and I surveyed our alternatives; I felt impelled to make good on my threat. Since the Long Beach office would not intercede with the Eleventh Naval District commandant in our behalf, it required little genius to conclude that we had two options: submit or act for ourselves. At my suggestion we tossed a coin to determine which one of us would venture to San Diego to plead the case personally (certainly not Navy protocol).

The chain-of-command for such communication was through the Long Beach office, but at that point even the thought of defying the system excited me. I knew that, if I journeyed to the city the sailors fondly called "Dago" (to the discomfiture of the city fathers) and failed to achieve my goal, I would at least enjoy the satisfaction of telling off someone who desperately needed correction; I wasn't sure that the captain was that sanguine. Never did I want to win a coin toss so badly. Whoever originated that message needed to know the facts so that he could either reverse his action or take my verbal abuse.

I won and was off by Greyhound at my own expense. During a brief lay-over at Capistrano, I ordered a piece of cherry pie and a glass of milk to kill time. I couldn't appreciate the spectacle of the historic Spanish mission next to the bus terminal or think about the visiting swallows because my mind was focused only on the unknown who seemed determined to foul up my summer schedule.

On the final leg of the trip, the bus delivered me within walking distance of Broadway Pier, the closest Navy installation which fortunately housed the information center. Presenting my copy of the fateful radio message to the clerk, I asked to be directed to the office that originated it. After several intermediate stops, I was ushered into the office of Commander Hesser and poured out my complaint interspersed with a little bitterness. Before my verbal castigation of the order reached its climax, the commander interrupted and completely disarmed me by apologetically pointing out that his record did not indicate that the 145 had already begun the decommissioning process. Of course, that information was accurate, but I deliberately omitted the fact that only informal approval had been given to remove certain types of light equipment.

The commander explained that he had requested the transfer to San Diego only because the record showed that we had been in port for an extended period without any visible strides toward decommissioning. On learning that part of the ship's gear had already been dispatched ashore, he complimented me as "a young officer with foresight" who "shelled out" his own money to correct a Navy miscue. How angry could I be after that?

In charge of all amphibious vessels in a Naval District that included Long Beach, Commander Hesser signed the name of his boss, the commandant, to all of his decisions, thus giving them the endorsement of a vice admiral. Wielding such power, he was seldom challenged, and that may account for the Long Beach reluctance to intervene in our behalf; fortunately for me he accepted my appeal.

Apparently I overwhelmed him almost as much as he overwhelmed me. Impressed by my initiative in calling the ill-timed transfer of the 145 to his attention, he offered me a job on his staff to be effective as soon as our ship was decommissioned. To make the assignment more attractive, he proposed an immediate advancement in rank (which he could arrange) if I agreed, but I declined. Then he added that, if I preferred to take my accumulated leave and return as a civilian to take charge of all decommissioned amphibious ships, he could accept that alternative. Again I declined, but my refusal did not deter him from sending a message to Long Beach canceling our transfer to San Diego.

I thanked him profusely for understanding our plight, and before I left he added: "If you change your mind about my offer or if I can ever do anything for you, let me know." With that parting verbal pat-on-the-back, he concluded: "I like smart, aggressive officers." Apparently paying my way from Long Beach simply to redress a wrong had registered an indelible impression; he was still unaware that my summer school plan, not an unfortunate Navy order, had prompted my action.

At the Capistrano bus stop, enroute back to the ship, I was more concerned about the swallows that stopped there in season; in fact, I was so exhilarated with my accomplishment that I felt as though I too were flying.

Word of my success preceded me; the commander's radioed order reached the ship before my arrival. To crew members committed as I was to mothballing the ship as quickly as possible, I became a momentary hero. While we aboard the 145 rejoiced in our good fortune, no one at the Long Beach base was laughing. They had no clue concerning how the Navy chain-of-command had been breached, and I was not about to gloat in their presence. Realizing that our call for a new deal had been mysteriously answered, they decided to teach us a lesson. Although I didn't appreciate it at the time, I also had a trump card of my own remaining.

178

The base decided that it would no longer honor our special privilege of remaining at the pier while other LSMs complained about being forced to anchor in the harbor. Without further explanation the 145 was ordered to the most remote part of the bay. Again I asked to see the chief who had been feasting on our steaks and butter, but he continued to be unavailable to speak in our behalf. We had no alternative but to comply with the order. Liberty was still possible but less convenient because we again had to rely on a harbor shuttle a la Pearl Harbor. As the 145 swung at anchor, removal of additional gear to the storage locker was halted, and summer school seemed remote once again, but I didn't stop conniving.

After fretting and seething for a week, I recalled Commander Hesser's invitation to let him know if he could assist me in any way. Willing to reach for any straw in what I was coming to regard as a losing duel with the Long Beach base, I boarded another bus for San Diego to make a second call on the commander. To his misfortune, he was in the office to hear my newest complaint. Using our banishment to the far corner of the harbor as my basic evidence, I explained that we were being shafted because he had reversed the order so that we could remain at Long Beach. As delicately as possible I tried to tell him that I now preferred to be ordered to San Diego for decommissioning.

Leaning back in his chair, the commander uttered a few religious words out of context. Then he jerked his chair to an upright position, and looking me in the eye, blurted out: "Let me get this straight. You came down here last week to ask me to cancel an order?" Almost before I could admit that to be fact, he continued: "You are sitting before me today asking me to cancel the cancellation?" With that he had captured the essence of my request, and I could only reply with a simple "Yes, sir." He leaned back, cussed with a little more gusto, then stood up and declared. "If I do that, the Long Beach bunch will think that I'm nuts." He paused and then added: "But for you I'll do it. I know they'll think I'm mad." Reminded that the ship had been stripped of so much gear that we could not possibly make the trip under our own power, he arranged to have us towed.

Leaving the commander's office, I felt satisfied with myself. Outside his door I encountered his attractive, exquisitely dressed civilian secretary who manifested more than a modicum of southern charm when she spoke: "You can't say that I don't work for the kindest man in the Navy. I've seen people thrown out of there for one-tenth of what you got away with." I readily agreed that her boss was most magnanimous in his understanding of my problem.

Although I had not fully overlooked this beauty on my way in, she was secondary to my mission; but now I had the presence of mind to add: "Since you seem to have overheard our conversation, you know that I will be in town on Thursday evening. I'm unacquainted with San Diego. Would you consider having dinner with me that evening and showing me a little of the city?" Emily agreed, and we met in the lobby of the US Grant Hotel. After dinner we walked for more than an hour before I escorted her home via trolley from the Santa Fe station to a house on Fairmount Street where she lived with an elderly couple. This began a relationship that brightened my San Diego experience.

The next morning Emily reported the evening's event to Commander Hesser, and as if by magic, I was instantly transformed into his fair-haired boy. As I had learned in the conversation the night before, Emily had followed her sailor-husband from Baton Rouge to San Diego where she found employment with Commander Hesser. Shortly thereafter her husband was shipped overseas only to become a casualty aboard a carrier. An empathetic commander quickly became Emily's self-proclaimed protector. That was a full two years before I was "towed" into their lives. To the commander's knowledge Emily had registered no interest in any young man, and none had invited her out until I asked her to dinner at the Grant. After that, invitations and acceptances became a routine.

One evening we took a bus to LaJolla to hear an outrageous concert by the Spike Jones Band; the finale featured a number entitled "Leave the Dishes in the Sink, Mirandy" that made no one's Hit Parade. As the band played, a percussionist with hammer in hand methodically broke a set of dishes in time with the music.

On other occasions we took in movies, enjoyed an evening at the Ice Capades, or attended the opening of a shopping center on North Island where Commander Hesser invested in a hobby shop in anticipation of his own retirement. But no evening was more memorable and hilarious than our trip to Tijuana. The ubiquitous bus, the Navy man's most faithful servant on land, took us to the international border, where tourists had to walk a short distance across a no-man's land to the waiting cabs and vans that carried those who elected not to walk into town. As Em and I walked into Mexican territory, a quick glance told me that tourists far outnumbered taxis. When a cab came along, without a word to my companion, I ran ahead, jumping over a gutter to commandeer it before someone else did.

Emily, who had been in Tijuana before, knew the distance into town, and preferred to walk. By the time she had caught up with me, she stood on the opposite side of the ditch about fifteen feet away. Unable to be heard above the roar of the traffic and the hubbub of the crowd, she motioned to me to let the cab go and come back to the walkway. Not knowing the distance into town and attempting to be gallant, I was reluctant to surrender the cab. The driver added to the confusion; he encouraged me to go back, but insisted that he would wait; that seemed contradictory. Why wait if we were going to walk? Suddenly the pieces fell into place; Em was standing in front of a five-minute quickie wedding chapel; the driver thought that she wanted to get married and that I didn't. After a few more gesturing exchanges, we all "got on the same page;" the cabbie drove off, and the two of us walked into town, laughing all the way.

That evening in particular relieved the tedium of my final weeks in the Navy—with summer school almost absent from my mind. On the day that we shut down the ship's galley and ate our last meal aboard, I invited Commander Hesser and Emily to join us for lunch in the wardroom. The occasion was light and merry although the commander decided to mix business with pleasure. He asked the captain and me to evaluate the efficiency of his decommissioning staff in working with our crew. We had to admit that the few delays that occurred were our responsibility because everyone in the ship's company who could type had already been discharged on points; consequently our invoices, approximately 500 in number, were being hammered out by sailors who regarded the typewriter as a complex gadget that defied the talents of a skilled deckhand.

With this revelation as his cue, the commander interrupted; turning to Emily, he asked: "Do you have any pressing work this afternoon?" Quizzically shaking her head, she asked for an explanation. "Good," he exclaimed, "You can stay and type for the boys this afternoon, provided the exec treats you to dinner tonight," a proposal that he knew had already been accepted. Emily stayed.

On a typing table rigged on the tank deck, she demonstrated the proper technique and gave a professional touch to our invoices. Meanwhile the commander had been escorted ashore in possession of all the medicinal liquor (two partial bottles) that remained aboard.

Once back at the office, he was repeatedly questioned about Emily's absence. Each time he answered a query, he embellished it a little more until his imagination and devilish instincts (of which I was totally oblivious over the preceding days) were in high gear. He informed one member of his staff that Emily so enjoyed life aboard the 145 that she contemplated a transfer. That comment caused a bright light to go on in his mind; he sat down and filled out a regular Navy transfer form (with the seven traditional copies with which Emily was familiar) sending her to the LSM 145 "as cabin girl third class for whatsoever duties the executive officer should assign." The order was countersigned by Commodore Sloat, the commander's immediate superior, along with a directive sending her to sick bay for a physical examination to determine if she were qualified for transfer.

When Emily reported for work the next morning, this "official" document was in the center of her desk. She considered it the product of a perverted mind, but believed she had to share knowledge of "the transfer" with someone. Because of Commander Hesser's planned absence, she was forced to seek an explanation from Commodore Sloat, with whom all her previous contacts had been strictly business. Seated at his desk, ramrod erect and formal, he fielded her question about the document to which his signature was affixed and without the hint of a smile answered: "Yes, my dear, your boss is quite a prankster."

On that morning of Emily's "impending re-assignment," the United States was transferring six LSTs to Chiang Kai-shek's Nationalist Government. A Chinese admiral was on the base to finalize the deal with Commander Hesser because of his control over all amphibious vessels in the District. Even as he concluded the paperwork, the commander did not forget that a small part of his prank was still incomplete.

He informed the visiting Chinese dignitary that a US Navy car would chauffeur him to the dock where the LSTs, now officially assigned to China, were nested, but explained that on the way the driver must stop and deliver "an urgent message" to the LSM 145.

By chance I was on deck when the black limo stopped, and the driver came up the gangway asking for Lieutenant Kehl. (I had been promoted some months before.) Not privy at this point to any part of the commander's practical joke, I apprehensively opened the official-looking envelope. Inside was a carbon copy of the memorandum ordering Emily to the 145 as cabin girl third class. Relieved that the Navy did not want to punish me for past "sins," I attended to the final chores of decommissioning in a relaxed mood except for the final night.

I returned to the ship about midnight from seeing Emily only to remember that during the day my mattress and all the bedding had fallen victim to the decommissioning process and were removed to storage. Confronted with the two insufferable alternatives of sleeping on the cold, steel deck or on the bare, metal springs of my bunk, I opted for the latter. Within a few minutes I was painfully aware that my career at sea was ending

184

on a Medieval torture rack; even during the worst of the typhoons my sleep had not been so unceremoniously impeded. No matter how I turned, those ubiquitous metal strips kept using me as a human pin cushion.

By morning I was thoroughly beat, but as I pondered the day ahead, the adrenalin began to pump, and the night on the rack quickly faded into memory. At mid-morning the simple, but highly symbolic, decommissioning officially took place; consisting of four parts, it was basically a flag ceremony. Most meaningful to the individual crew members was the Navy tradition surrounding the homing pennant.

When a ship that had been on station overseas for an extended period received orders back to the States, it announced its destination by unfurling from its yardarm a flag distinctive to the occasion. Comprised of a white star on a blue field for every officer who had been overseas for at least a year, followed by a red and white streamer as many feet long as the number of sailors who had served abroad for a similar period, the flag of the 145 was sewn together before we left Guam. With stars for the captain and me, our streamer was about eighteen feet long, and we proudly displayed it especially on entering Pearl Harbor, Long Beach, and San Diego.

Now was the time to haul down our homing pennant and cut it up, giving a part of the streamer to each eligible enlisted man and a star to the appropriate officers. That was followed by a lowering of both the American flag and the Union Jack. After that the final step in the symbolism was the removal of the commission pennant that had flown, uninterrupted although tattered, at the top of the mast from commissioning on June 12, 1944, to that day, May 22, 1946. This seventy-two-inch pennant measured three inches in width where attached to the ship, but tapered to one inch at the other end. The first eighteen inches consisted of seven white stars with a blue background followed by a fifty-four-inch red and white streamer.

Detaching this pennant signified that the 145 was no longer a part of the active fleet, and to legalize the transfer Commander Hesser was on hand to take over control of the vessel from the captain and formally end his responsibility. After the ceremony we bid farewell to each other and went our separate ways. I met Emily for lunch and then headed for the airport and a cross-country flight home.

A romantic climax to these final four months of Navy duty would have sent Emily and me to the altar before the end of the year. I'm sure that Commander Hesser was already planning to give the bride away, but fate decreed otherwise. After promising to visit Emily later in the summer at her Baton Rouge home, where she planned to vacation, I flew to Philadelphia and my discharge from active duty. Returning home, I was overwhelmed with a whirl of activities—renewing acquaintances, swapping stories with friends who had also served in the armed forces, and attending the summer school program that had prompted my impatience with Navy procedures over those last months.

Before the summer ended, the University of Pittsburgh offered me a teaching assistantship, and I never found time to visit Louisiana before assuming that assignment. Emily and I corresponded, but for both of us absence made the heart grow fonder for someone else. Gradually the letters stopped. After a hiatus of more than thirty years, I received a letter from Emily, who coincidentally was living around the corner from a friend of mine whom she knew. Pleasantly surprised to hear from her, I was also overjoyed to know that someone alive out there could vouch for much of what had happened during those final four months in the Navy. Over the years, as I reminisced about those incidents, I'm sure that some of my friends thought I had been out in the sun too long or had imbibed too much bad tequila. It was a relief to note that my tales, seemingly embellished, could be verified.

Emily's letter began: "I have been working for some time in the Economics Department at the University of Colorado. The other day my thoughts drifted to you. I pulled down the *Dictionary of American Scholars* to see if you had persevered in your ambition to become a college professor. Having found your name and address, I decided to drop you a note."

A Reminder

To

Those Civilians Who Manned the Ships

. . . a job well done—a job of which you can be proud as long as you live because it gave mankind another opportunity to live together in peace and decency.

James V. Forrestal
Secretary of the Navy

ABOUT THE AUTHOR

James A. Kehl was born in and educated in Pennsylvania, receiving his B.A. and M.A. from the University of Pittsburgh and his Ph.D. from the University of Pennsylvania. Called to active duty in the Navy in February 1944, he served as an officer aboard "LSM 911." In 1946 he began a long and distinguished teaching career as a professor of history, primarily at the University of Pittsburgh, that concluded with his appointment as Professor Emeritus in 1992. For eleven of those years, including four as Dean of the College of Arts and Science, he also served as a university administrator. During his career he was tapped to such honor societies as Omicron Delta Kappa, Phi Alpha Theta, and Phi Eta Sigma and received a Distinguished Alumnus Award from the university and a Meritorious Service Award from Phi Alpha Theta for his work as a national officer. Jim Kehl's other books include *Ill Feeling in the Era of Good Feeling*; and *Boss Rule in the Gilded Age*; his articles have appeared in numerous scholarly publications. Dr. Kehl lives in Pittsburgh with his wife, Barbara.